MANAGING
COMPANY-WIDE
COMMUNICATION

MANAGING COMPANY-WIDE COMMUNICATION

WERNER DAVID

Management Consultant

London and New York

CHAPMAN & HALL

University and Professional Division

London · Glasgow · Weinheim · New York · Tokyo · Melbourne · Madras

Published by Chapman & Hall, 2–6 Boundary Row, London SE1 8HN, UK

Chapman & Hall, 2–6 Boundary Row, London SE1 8HN, UK

Blackie Academic & Professional, Wester Cleddens Road, Bishopbriggs, Glasgow G64 2NZ, UK

Chapman & Hall GmbH, Pappelalle 3, 69469 Weinheim, Germany

Chapman & Hall USA, One Penn Plaza, 41st Floor, New York NY 10119, USA

Chapman & Hall Japan, ITP-Japan, Kyowa Building, 3F, 2-2-1 Hirakawacho, Chiyoda-ku, Tokyo 102, Japan

Chapman & Hall Australia, Thomas Nelson Australia, 102 Dodds Street, South Melbourne, Victoria 3205, Australia

Chapman & Hall India, R. Seshadri, 32 Second Main Road, CIT East, Madras 600 035, India

First edition 1995

© 1995 Werner David

Typeset in 11/13pt Bembo by Saxon Graphics Ltd., Derby
Printed in Great Britain by T.J. Press (Padstow) Ltd., Padstow, Cornwall

ISBN 0 412 56420 3

A catalogue record for this book is available from the British Library

∞ Printed on permanent acid-free text paper, manufactured in accordance with ANSI/NISO Z39.48–1992 and ANSI/NISO Z39.48–1984

CONTENTS

Contents

1

COMMUNICATE AND WIN

How a company or any organization is first built and then maintained by communication. The function is recognized to be a discrete and continuing task at every level. A Communication Health Index helps to monitor effectiveness.

INTRODUCTION

Communication is a motor that can never be stopped. It is the function that drives the endless cycle of activity: building and maintaining understanding, capturing attention and persuading.

The concept is clear and generally accepted but in practice the mention of communication all too often gets reactions such as: 'They really have a lot to learn', 'It is very poor with us', 'Nobody knows what is going on'. Alternatively, there is bewilderment that this need be an agenda item, even resentment that the adequacy of something so fundamental to management and the daily routine need be questioned.

How is it that an activity in which everyone participates is nevertheless so often found wanting? Why do people who are in constant contact so often find, and then only when disaster strikes, that they have not understood one another? How can organizations fail so completely to manage the communication function that they collapse while others, operating in the same field, continue to build and grow?

Two simple precepts underlie the understanding and effective use of communication:

- it is a **continuous** function, to be directed consciously (even total silence communicates);
- **everyone**, from the recruit to the senior director, has a role in the communication network.

Communication is one area of management not subject to chance. This book is a structured and practical guide to the development of the ability to communicate, by individuals and within organizations, using proven techniques.

Data is always incomplete

At the same time, it has to be recognized that no matter how well communication is managed, data and intelligence are seldom if ever complete. People are talking, reading and writing, listening and watching during every waking moment. The demand for more information is insatiable but the data available on any subject at any given point is unlikely to be comprehensive. In practice, activity has to continue, and plans and decisions are made in the face of uncertainties.

There is, therefore, a strong incentive to use fully the information that exists and to capture that which is readily obtainable. Continuing experience (and some of the outstanding cases will be studied) proves how failure to do one or the other, or both, has resulted at the minimum in the loss of valuable resource but has often also ultimately proved to be fatal.

Winning by communicating starts with identification of the function as a discrete task, at every level in the organization. This is followed by the building and maintenance of a network linking each element of the organization.

THE COMMUNICATION NETWORK ELEMENTS

The elements making up the integrated company-wide network are shown in Table 1.1.

While the importance of sound communication is usually accepted in theory, the evidence of decades of direct experience with managements worldwide is that:

- the effort to build an integrated network is casual and often spasmodic;
- appreciation of network communication declines with seniority.

The reasons – and excuses – for the negligent management of communications are many. For instance, issues are often not clear-cut and the natural reaction of management is to say nothing until a decision is made. Often managers place emphasis on a self-defined image, and the belief develops that only 'good' news need be told. Unfortunately, the 'bad' news can then become gossip – that potent sap of morale and dissipation of effort.

Table 1.1 The elements of an integrated company network

Area	Segment	Group
External	Market	Individual client All potential by 'cell' (age, income, interest, etc.)
	Environment	Political/legislative Pressure groups (incl. local communities, the media)
	Finance	Shareholders/partners Institutions Banks
	Suppliers	Services (e.g. agencies, auditors) Goods/materials
Internal		Every employee Staff groups/unions

Another factor inhibiting communication is that, while discussion can only be realistic and relevant if based on current data, the wider publication of information, even internally, can have statutory implications for executives. On the one hand it is an offence to mislead the financial markets and, on the other, no opportunity can be given for knowledge being used for insider trading. Most commonly, however, senior managers, busy and believing themselves to be informed, can lose understanding of and sympathy with the anxiety or desire for enlightenment elsewhere.

In these circumstances, communication as such is not part of the daily routine. The result is that in practical terms, management has no forum for contact with the workforce and fails to exploit all the available talent, while the employees feel remote and even alienated from the organization.

Communication effectiveness is measurable. Empirically, a satisfactory state of affairs is reflected in the level of casual contact and a general perspective of being involved, of eagerness to contribute. Professionally, a Communication Health Index is built to measure the overall state of communication and also to identify specific shortcomings.

BUILDING EFFECTIVE COMMUNICATION

Identification of the key role of communication is the first step in building the function into a winning tool.

Responsibilities

A director or senior manager is given the responsibility for linking every employee into the communication network. It then remains a continuing task to ensure that each individual cooperates to the full and, in turn, is satisfied with the data received, specifically for the job but also on the state of affairs generally.

Training

People have to be built into communicators by encouragement and training. Office politics are inevitable but can be harnessed to achieve cooperation.

Building the network

The communication network is built on all available media and places particular emphasis on monitoring the market for change. The intricacies of communicating beyond the home market and internationally are identified, for use to best advantage. The network also ensures constructive links with regulatory, environmental and special-issue interests. Provision is made for handling disaster.

Monitoring the network

Communication is as subject to change as everything else and the network requires continuous monitoring and auditing to ensure its effective functioning and that no barriers are built to restrict the flow of data and intelligence. Market research and public relations are important tools in running the network and for monitoring its effectiveness. These professional skills are used in building the Communication Health Index.

Costing communication

Communication can be costed. Certain definitions need to be agreed and a pro-forma budget can then be developed for the function across the organization. Such an overview provides a basis for managing the network. It is also another insight into the corporate structure as a whole.

2

SCOPE OF THE NETWORK

The switch from hierarchical communication to the network. The traditional pattern with information passing up and operational instruction flowing down the line is replaced by continuous two-way contact between all elements of the organization.

INTRODUCTION

Effective communication begins with an assessment of the existing situation. What data is being delivered to management, department, function and each individual and what is expected in return? How much of the data becomes useful information? Conversely, what are the perceived needs that are not being met now? Then, importantly, what information needs are not even recognized?

THE WEAKNESS OF HIERARCHICAL COMMUNICATION

The traditional structure of communication is, in essence, for information to pass upwards, in formal reports and by way of meetings and presentations. In turn, instruction flows back to the operating units and the front-line workers.

This hierarchical pattern of communication (Figure 2.1) has a number of weaknesses:

- the further down the line, the less the involvement. The 'shop floor', the great majority, work only with data sufficient for the task in hand and are not expected to make further contribution;
- at best, the organization is failing to reach and tap the full potential of the employees, at worst the majority are alienated;

- management is in danger of isolation, becoming remote not only internally but also from the marketplace;
- and, perhaps most importantly, a fixed, rigid pattern of communication can result in failure to monitor, and perhaps to be ignorant of change.

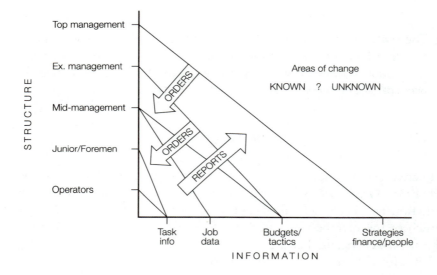

Figure 2.1 The hierarchical pattern of communication.

This one-way flow of communication reflects a splintered organization. Top management is remote from the work force and also uncertain, possibly ignorant, and at worst arrogantly uncaring of what is happening 'outside'. There is no structure for employees in the lower levels, the junior manager, the foreman and the operator, to maintain contact with the top floor offices. The great majority are uncertain of what is happening, do not feel involved nor see themselves as integral to the enterprise. In the circumstances both sides lose and, eventually, so will the shareholder (and perhaps the pensioner).

The 'outside' is made up of the ever-looming 'areas of change'. The imperative of staying in touch with what is happening in the industry, in the immediate ambience, is usually recognized but there are also the 'areas of the unknown'. The ever-increasing tempo of change means that an unrelated technological breakthrough can bring devastation.

At one extreme, it took the jet airliner perhaps a decade to destroy ocean-going passenger shipping; at the other, the advent of a milk-inducing hormone, greatly increasing milk production, now threatens every small dairy herd in the advanced world.

THE MANAGED COMMUNICATION NETWORK

The scope of managed communication is entirely different. As Figure 2.2 shows, the aim is for communication to run across the structure, binding the organization and reaching out to monitor both the known and unknown 'areas of change'.

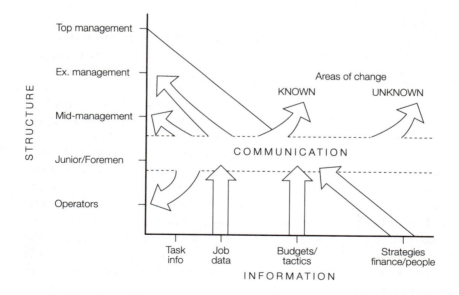

Figure 2.2 The pattern of network communication.

The study of management has itself become an 'industry' – and a growth one at that, with a bewildering output of theories, exhortations and insights. No sooner does a leading teacher, such as Tom Peters, update thinking than three leading Harvard Business School teachers, Robert Eccles, Nitin Nohria and James Berkley in their book *Beyond the Hype* suggest that there is little if anything 'new' in these ever-evolving ideas.[1]

Recent examples of poor communication in industry

In practice, the experience of public utilities since their change by privatization into commercial corporations offers valuable guidance to management needs – and communication is shown to have a pivotal role. In a press interview some four years after the change at his company, Trevor Newton, group managing director of Yorkshire Water in the UK, still found the management style too hierarchial, with **little information flow except from top to bottom**.

He commented: 'Communication between employees and managers is poor, achievement often goes unrewarded and ideas still largely come from the top ... [now] ideas are starting to flow up management lines instead of down and managers are learning to recognize and reward good work.'

With these changes came a radical restructuring of the organization centred on the identification of the core and peripheral functions, and other activities were contracted.

A classic example of how failure to communicate, both internally and with the outside 'areas of unknown change', overwhelmed an organization was that of Rolls Royce, the engineering company at the heart of industrial Britain. Here a board, blinded by technology, failed to collect the necessary intelligence or to listen to and absorb the data on the implications of their investment programme in new engines until, unbelievably, bankruptcy was upon them. These experienced men were so cocooned by eminence and decades of success as to be deaf to all but the enthusiasm of a new generation's technology; technology which they possibly did not fully understand. Crucially, the lines of communication stopped short of any other input, particularly that of finance, and were closed to an unknown area, where the market and the world were changing. It is a story to be read almost daily in the newspapers.

In Germany, the traditional secrecy of management has been thrown into question by the spectacular collapse, and last-minute rescue of Metallgesellschaft, one of the country's top industrial groups. The cause, a large loss on futures trading by a US subsidiary, has revealed a yawning communication gap between the executive and the supervisory board.

Although made up of top industrial and trade union figures, this body, responsible in law for large expenditures, only became aware of the disaster after the event. Shareholders have learned that the group of over 250 operating units had no integrated communication network.

Information is of the essence in business, a principle so obvious that the state and art of communication is not subjected to the routine scrutiny devoted to more measurable functions, such as finance, marketing effectiveness and production efficiency – although in the final analysis it is the ability to capture and use data and intelligence that governs success or prevents disaster.

Communication as the nerve system of organizations

As an analogy, the nervous system is the communication network of the body. The nerves are not an obvious part of the anatomy but a function failure of the system is felt at once. The nerves are not as open to treatment as are more physical elements, the heart or the lungs, yet they will receive equal attention from the health care specialist. Medicine recognizes that life is built on a healthy and fully functioning nervous system.

The conclusion is clear: a routine task for every manager is the monitoring of the state of communication within his or her area of responsibility. It is no different and as germane to success as the measurement of results against budget or researching the impact of the marketing effort.

THE CONTACT CHANNELS

From the dawn of history, communication and the development of a society based on barter and trade went hand-in-hand. The first early human to hawk a skin had to learn that the item had a value, find the person and the place where this value was recognized and then communicate the desirability of the surplus against the usefulness of salt, fruit or whatever was desired in exchange. Certainly it would not have been long before the skin trader could distinguish drier salt and fresher fruit, but by then there were also cleaner, bigger skins on offer from other hunters seeking improved salt and fruit.

Every step was and is governed by the ability to establish and use a communication network. The process must have developed step-by-step, from individual word-of-mouth to group contact, up to the modern media that has the capability to link every individual. Three distinct areas of contact exist, and each needs to be reviewed by a manager in terms of objectives.

Personal communication

In private, person-to-person exchange is usually haphazard or casual. In the business environment, it is both casual and arranged and planned. In social life, letter-writing plays a part but since the advent of the telephone and the terminal, this delightful medium has become marginal. On the other hand, in business, the writing of reports and memos are key organizational communication skills and electronic contact and networking is resulting in another explosion of the 'written' word.

Public communication

Much of public data, the provision of 'news' by the print media, radio and television, is useful information, but is not directly relevant to the recipient. Nevertheless, it has many implications both for the individual and the organization. Events in the world at large, and economic and environmental developments, create both opportunities and difficulties.

Media 'noise' is in the main generalized, with writers and editors often having to make assumptions about the interests of their public. More directly of interest are the specialist channels – print, broadcasting and electronic data – that are designed to meet specific information needs. An important element of the communication network is the ability to monitor, within finite time and resources, the relevant material from all that is publicly available.

Organizational communication

A managed structure, the communication network, is required if all the information available internally and coming to hand during the course of business, is to be used effectively. In essence, organizational communication has two functions:

- internally – to keep informed and maintain motivating contact with each employee; in turn, for each individual to be in a position to join in and contribute ideas and suggestions and to comment on change;
- externally – both to reach as many as possible of those who make up the market or target sectors of the population and also to monitor change.

The willing internal audience

Potential customers are often reluctant listeners and, in consequence, much effort is devoted to identifying with, and to be seen as meeting, the needs of the audience. However, the existence of the same imperative for internal communication must also be recognized: in-house communication is not the Cinderella of all activity, to be given occasional and cursory attention, but is a task requiring the same attention, thought and effort as every other.

In order to reach the external market, advertising and promotional effort is usually created and run with the help of professional staff and agencies. It is not always recognized that a level of commitment and professional planning is also required to meet internal communication needs. It is not enough for management to be satisfied with the use of professional expertise to produce, say, the company magazine, but fail to employ and put in place the specialist arrangements necessary for the running and maintenance of the communication network. The central nerve system cannot be left to work by itself, unrecognized until something goes wrong or there is a disaster.

The external disinterest

It is salutory to remember that until well into recorded time, communication was virtually confined to direct contact: what could be said and seen, heard and felt between individuals and small groups, living in relative isolation. Distant events and developments might have no impact in a lifetime, whole civilizations rose and fell unknown outside their geographic confines.

The reverse side of the coin was that in such circumstances, without information and the ability to communicate widely and use intelligence from afar, people were unable to take precautions against developing dangers – a plague or an invasion would arrive without warning from the 'areas of the unknown' and devastate the unprepared.

The advent of mass communication has not eliminated the unforeseen, and disaster can and does strike down what may seem the best of plans, but more often than not, the cause can be traced to a faulty system, to failure to ensure first the availability and then the use of accurate information. With the accelerating tempo of change, it is the ability to continue collecting, handling and using data that is the foundation stone of business and organizational success – and indeed of survival.

SILENCE ALSO COMMUNICATES

Silence can be a tempting and apparently easy option, but it also tells a story. Increasingly in the modern environment, it is one of irresolution and lack of structure, a hint of disinterest and of decline and fall. A thoughtful commentary by an important Swiss bank describes silence as static, and goes on to say:

> A Latin proverb cautions the chatterer: 'If you had said nothing you would still be a philosopher'. Those who say nothing, however and do not expose themselves to the venture of Communication are captives of their own silence. At an elementary level, all life begins when the cells of one body or the elements of an ecological whole begin to communicate with each other. The venture of communication is the venture of life itself – far transcending the mere instrument of language (J. Vontobel).[2]

Each organization, corporation and company develops a culture, a way of doing things, which tends towards the routine and the status quo, and carries within itself the danger of creeping inertia. A sound communication network provides the tools for adapting to the realities of continuous change, to keeping pace with and improving upon what is happening in the marketplace. By providing accurate and timely data, a communication network makes deliberate choice possible, allows the achievement of optimum results from available resources.

In parallel, an efficient communication network is built to allow the unusual, innovative, maverick idea or comment to be heard.

Communication does not simply move up and down line management – the network links all functions and new thinking is not only allowed but is encouraged to jump rigid departmental lines and established reporting structures.

THE MONITORS OF BUSINESS

Business is monitored and assessed by audits. First and best-known is the regular statutory financial scrutiny of the accounts and balance sheet. Less obvious are the continuing assessments, backed by ever more stringent legal imperatives, of the various inspectorates and of the ubiquitous 'green' and consumer groups. These all set out to check on the environmental impact of what is being done, on quality and standards, on the terms and conditions applied to operations.

It is to be recognized that the communication network also requires periodic, formal state-of-health check. The basis is the 'audit' of each element of the network linking the operational areas (Chapter 11). For the organization to be able to 'sign off' in all areas implies successful communication, with:

- the market;
- the sources of finance;
- the suppliers;
- political, statutory and environmental interests;

and, in parallel, maintaining the internal network from which the rest in fact flows.

SUMMARY

Network communication replaces the hierarchical pattern. Internally, the network provides channels for two-way contact between every level of the organization.

Equally, the network is designed to link the organization with its environment. A primary aim is to monitor change, both that perceived in the specific segment but also more widely in 'areas of unknown change'.

The network uses every channel of personal, public and organizational communication and is as subject to 'audit' as every other aspect of the operation.

REFERENCES

1. Eccles, R., Nohria, N. and Berkley, J. (1992) *Beyond the Hype*, Harvard Business School Press.
2. Vontobel, J. (1989) *Communication: A Corporate Venture*, Annual Report, Zurich.

3

ESTABLISHING THE FORMAL COMMUNICATION NETWORK

The basis of effective communication is the commitment of top management. Building the network starts with assessing and defining the gaps in the existing structure. This chapter goes on to describe the formal network that is then built on the annual cycle of meetings, conferences and visits and on the reporting structure and notes the function of the central desk.

INTRODUCTION

As with any activity, successful and effective communication is planned, constructed and managed. There is one useful difference: establishing a communication network does not involve capital investment or further overhead in management costs. The communication objective can be achieved by the mobilization of resources that already exist or can readily be aligned by any organization. It is an asset that is waiting to be exploited, given only the will and management talent so to do.

CREATING THE ENVIRONMENT

Communication is an intangible; to work effectively, the function needs to be understood and operated in a sympathetic environment. Every organization has a history and culture, reflected in current working practices but during any given period, the chief executive, whether at divisional, company or group level, has a pervasive impact. It is his or her attitude that is directly reflected by the state and health of the communication function.

The chief officer and his board or management committee create the ambience: if there is to be effective company-wide communication these executives must be seen to be open to information, proposals and ideas and, in turn, show determination to share their thoughts and plans, and the news of results and achievements, with their fellows.

The White House and members of the American Congress can get millions of messages and comments on a single issue; it is a simple test of communication effectiveness for a company chief to ask him- or herself – how many contacts, messages, comments do I receive from outside the formal line structure? Perhaps the answer is: none (or even, that none is wanted!).

If that is the case, the wealth of talent that lies within the workforce, the advisers and consultants and in the marketplace is not being fully tapped. It is a rare person who when given the opportunity to put forward his or her ideas – and is sure of being recognized – will not do so willingly and eagerly. The mechanism of, and the motivation for, communication have to be put in place. The flow will not self-start but, once established, will bring continuing reward in terms of heightened commitment and a stream of ideas and proposals.

Assessing existing structures and needs

A factual survey establishes what is **currently being delivered**. While the collection of data is necessarily structured by unit in any but the smallest enterprise, it is possible for the results to be set out schematically, showing the data flow from and to each individual. Although many will have identical involvement and can be banded in groups, such as by category of floor worker or by type of sales force or of technicians, the perception is of how the individual is kept in touch and, in turn can make contact.

The next step is to establish, by discussion group, through the use of professional research and by individual contact, the **perceived gaps**, i.e. the needs not being met by the existing structure.

In parallel, it is a task of management to assess the existing **interface with the market** and to make a judgment as to its adequacy.

Important extension of this review is the consideration of the 'areas of unknown change'. Here the network will mesh with strategic planning or, where such does not exist, help to lay the basis for the introduction of long-range planning.

Management for the network

The building and maintaining of a company-wide communication network must be the direct responsibility of a senior executive or director. This has to be a person with the authority to ensure that procedures are followed where necessary, that formal material is complete and above all, that the system is kept fluid and dynamic.

Directors and vice-presidents of communication exist in many corporations and organizations but not only do the functions of these posts vary widely but they are subject to change. Often, the task of the communications chief is in fact that of editorial director of house publications. Possibly there is some liaison function with the public relations consultancy, also involving advice to management, but seldom does such an executive have responsibility for company-wide communication. That role has to lie at the top level.

An existing situation may well reflect historic practice. Some form of communication becomes necessary very early in the life of a company, as soon in fact as an office or enterprise begins activity or seeks markets outside the immediate neighbourhood. Company expansion often starts with the appointment of agents, by the making of arrangements with dealers, possibly by the licensing of manufacture, packaging or the use of the trademark or process. Before long the successful management is faced with a structure of some complexity which not only has to be monitored but also guided and motivated.

The easy face-to-face and personal contact of the early days has soon to be augmented by a communication network, haphazard links replaced by a structure built to harness resources and talents that can be scattered between markets and across countries.

Building the communication routine

A structure depends upon routine, particularly on the regular submission of data and reports. An early task for communication management is to ensure:

- data is prepared in **standard formats**;

- **definitions** are agreed and understood by everyone;
- **timetables** are established and then maintained.

In other words, a basic step is for the internal data to be received on a **continuous** basis, and that given established definitions, it is **complete** and **clear**. These criteria ensure that information is as **current** as possible.

The four requirements, that data are **continuous, complete, clear** and **current** are together known as the **4C Principle of Communication** (Figure 3.1). Certainly, the principle can be applied to formal internal requirements but the aim of communication management is to ensure that as far as possible the same standards apply to the collection of external data and to the flow of intelligence back through the network. The task is to build the **4C** principle into an integrated network.

The central desk

A key element of the communication network is the central desk. The chief executive of any sizeable unit has a staff, perhaps as small as one assistant, and the function becomes established routine. A first step is

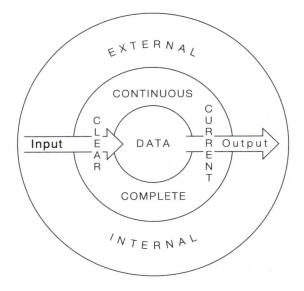

Figure 3.1 The routine of communication.

to arrange for all reports originating above a given level to be copied to the chief executive.

The central desk then checks both the 'secretarial' aspect – the timely receipt and correct format of the material – and the adequacy of the contents. It has the muscle to ensure compliance or can do so through the board director responsible for communication. Organization varies but the central desk can also be used to update the senior-level management databases, for example on personnel matters, competitive activity and market developments.

Such an arrangement clearly establishes responsibility for continuity and data integrity. A well-run central desk will ensure that individual units do not lose sight of a competitor, that technological developments are monitored, worldwide if necessary, and that in-house data are merged with commercially-available and public information.

The central desk is accessible by all managers as is appropriate, with data that can range from current production scheduling to details of the latest technical papers, world competitive status, industry news, legislative proposals. A seemingly endless list but once the reporting and monitoring structure is in place, it is not an onerous task to update central intelligence.

In reverse, the central desk has a key function in networking intelligence and in facilitating the flow of information around the organization.

ESTABLISHING THE FRAMEWORK

Effective communication requires a common framework for the routine of reporting and the cycle of formal contacts and meetings. This need can be met by a published policy manual. The temptation exists to hold the policy manual in distain, as bureaucratic and restrictive, but with experience comes appreciation of having to hand an unambiguous statement of the **operational framework** and of the **standards** expected of employees. The policy manual is both an administrative tool and an important element of the communication network.

The **operational framework** describes the routine administrative procedures, including the reporting requirements. These basic tools of management are set out by format, content and timing.

The **standards** for the business and its employees, the corporate rules of conduct, are also detailed in the manual. In this way, each member of the workforce is clear as to what is expected from her or him and, in the event of legal challenge or accident, the organization at least has evidence of the corporate intentions.

An effective manual is developed over time, and subject to change in the light of experience. It quickly becomes useful as an administrative tool in the elimination of day-to-day procedural queries and the misunderstandings that can be so wasteful of time and resource. Individual notes and memoranda, periodic instructions on policy are read, filed and forgotten in rapid succession – a waste of everyone's time. A policy manual, bound in hard covers that allow insertion of updates and amendments, stands to hand on a desk, available for reference on a daily basis.

One simple rule in the preparation of a manual, which also ensures clarity, is that policies are not discussed or explained but simply set down as requirements. For instance: 'the financial package will consist of ...' or 'the monthly report will be posted on the tenth working day of the month' are clear and unambiguous requirements. Explanations of why these procedures exist or of the reasoning behind them are confusing and add nothing to the usefulness of the manual as such.

Definitions

The basis of understanding and of avoiding confusion, is definition. Each term needs to be clear at every level in the organization and across geographic boundaries. Arriving at definitions can be a task of some complexity, the more so for international operations. Proof, if it were needed, of the value of a manual comes with its use as the organization's dictionary, defining every term of the industrial and in-house jargon.

Procter & Gamble, the multinational consumer-goods group, monitors the offtake of washing powder across markets by a standard unit of consumption. Progress can be watched worldwide without complicated adjustments for currency, packing, product variation. The standard unit of measurement also enables visitors to feel at home in any market.

The first definition in a manual can well be that for 'client' or 'customer'. There are often legal, technical or business-related reasons for defining the target customers. For instance, a specialist manufacturer with a policy of selling only to the trade and not the ultimate consumer will find it necessary to define 'trade'. There are restrictions in even the largest of consumer markets – perhaps the products can only be sold to adults, which is the case with cigarettes in many countries, or only after certain pre-conditions have been met, as with financial services.

It might be necessary to define 'a sale'. The market is not often that of 'everyone who can be persuaded to buy' and the analysis and thought involved in arriving at a full definition can be a salutory exercise, a focus on the whole concept of how the corporation views itself. Statements can be issued, aims declared but it is in the analytical process of creating definitions that operations have to be thought through and principles clarified.

Definitions can well change over time. For example, the product focus may widen or contract and then the re-definition itself becomes an element in the realignment of the enterprise to facing the new situation.

Marketing policies

The marketing section of the policy manual will set out the corporate rules of doing business. These will include:

- the principles underlying pricing;
- the qualifications for discounts;
- circumstances in which special services or products are available.

There will also be:

- rules governing third-party relationships;
- approval procedures for marketing programmes;
- and provision for any special features of the business.

The legal and legislative framework

An important section of the manual will be devoted to the legal and the moral framework for the business, that is the application to operations and to employees both of relevant law and of the accepted conventions and standards set for the industry.

Specifically, such law as the US Corrupt Practices Act or insider trader legislation and the relevant Code of Practice agreed by the professional or trade body are set out in terms of the daily routine. There can then be no misunderstandings: required behaviour is fully communicated and the manual is a ready point of reference.

Many corporations also develop their own statements of operational behaviour and the manual becomes a constant reminder of the standards expected from all employees.

Meetings and the annual cycle

Corporations and indeed all effective organizations operate on the basis of an annual round of meetings and conferences. The key event will be the planning and budget cycle but meetings might also be required for such functions as finance, production, legal and personnel. The manual can be the vehicle for establishing the due-dates for each stage of the budgeting cycle and for setting down the general routine of the year, a framework for individuals to plan their own working schedules.

Reports

The core of routine communication within an organization is the **financial package**. While a related handbook will deal with professional accounting principles, the policy manual will set out:

- management information requirements, ranging from the frequency of sales returns and cash forecasts to the periodic preparation of pro-forma balance sheets;
- procedures involved in obtaining approval for capital expenditures.

The format of each return is illustrated in the manual and a due-date laid down, requiring standard and timely financial communication from every branch and department of the organization.

Similarly, the policy manual will publish deadlines for the receipt of **market reports** and pro-formas illustrative of the requirements, e.g. for the sections covering such areas as sales and clients, market developments, competitive activity and technological change.

BUILDING THE MARKET COMMUNICATION LINKS

A key element of the communication network is the regular transmission of reports, in standard format, and a recognized flow of response (Figure 3.2).

The industry association

In most industrial sectors and increasingly for services, the industry, trade or professional association has important internal and external communication functions. In turn, the efficiency of the organization and its effectiveness is dependent on the measure of support given to it

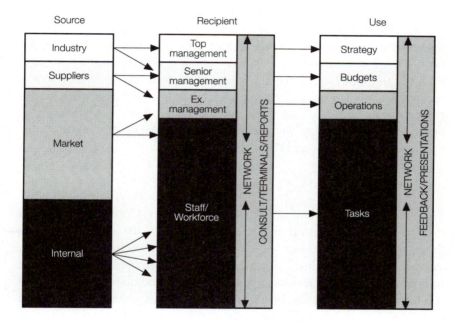

Figure 3.2 Main channels of data flow.

by the individual members, routinely and not during a crisis alone. Assessing the value of this link and maintaining it is a direct responsibility of the director holding the communication portfolio.

Externally, the association watches and is involved in the legal and environmental issues facing the membership (Chapter 12). However, the trade body is also an important source of data and intelligence, formally through newletters and briefings, informally by way of personal contact among the members. These data are usually fed into the corporation at senior management level, to the individuals sitting on committees and attending meetings.

In the company-wide communication environment, the recipients are responsible for feeding the information into the network. Association papers are circulated to those directly involved and summarized in the house journals and on the terminals. The 'news' that comes with personal contact, on developments in competitive companies, possible legislative and technological change, on the world scene, are all noted, allowing interested colleagues to follow up with personal enquiry. Reporting association activity becomes one of the routine reports fed into the system.

This channel of data input is likely to grow in importance as operating units become smaller, with greater self-management responsibilities. In such a structure, the individual unit, charged with a specific market task, does not have the capacity to look at the wider world outside and will need to be kept aware of what is happening in the environment. The role of trade bodies and industry associations is likely to grow in value as companies 're-engineer', cut 'back-room' management and concentrate on market specifics.

Suppliers

Suppliers are a valuable if informal source of data. Contact is usually at executive and buyer level and here individuals learn of what is being done by other companies, of market trends, of developments from 'outside' in terms both of related fields and of imports. A requirement to report formal contacts with suppliers, over and above the details of the buying arrangements, helps bring such intelligence into the house and heightens the overall awareness of the continuing need for everyone to communicate.

This requirement to report is not an extra burden, an added irritant, but should be seen as a valued contribution. It will be accepted as such if the contributions are recognized, perhaps discussed directly but certainly acknowledged. As a generality, suppliers are an under-used source of valuable data.

Liaison with agencies and partners

Much of the success of direct expansion, or through agency agreements, depends on the level and quality of the communication links between the offices or outside partners. In the case of the internal organization, requirements are set down in the policy manual but with third parties, it is helpful to establish the communication commitment on each side from the start. Failure to agree a structure, and it can be overlooked when other matters appear all-important, inevitably leads to difficulty, particularly if results should fail to meet expectations.

The essential routine written communication consists of:

- the **financial package**, including sales against budget and, where appropriate, stocks in hand;
- a **management report** on the operation or office;
- a **review** of the market situation.

Given no extraordinary circumstances, which need to be notified directly, a monthly return might well be sufficient.

In an agency relationship, each party agrees to keep the other informed of product problems, new developments and proposed changes. Normally, the principal will finance much if not all of the in-market promotional programme. By keeping control of communication within each market, the principal protects both the product or service identity and the market franchise.

Given that conditions change, and can do so rapidly, it is an important element of the relationship that communication be open, frank and timely. A delay in consulting or notifying a relevant development can be embarrassing and worse. Misunderstandings arise from assumptions, with one party believing that the other will have heard the news, be aware of what is happening in regard to an important development, forgetting that those not immediately involved can well have a different perspective.

Third World markets provide many direct examples of the hiatus caused by ill-considered and bewildering changes in regulations. At the height of the oil boom, a lifting of controls led every agency and trader involved with construction in Nigeria to order cement. The facts were known in-market but nothing was communicated until an armada of ships had arrived outside Lagos. There was chaos for months.

The boom faded and manufacturers who continued to ship goods to the country found that, no matter what the documentation, the lack of foreign exchange meant, at best, long-delayed payment. The well-informed supplied only against cash. Similar confusion exists in the countries of the former Soviet Union and is likely to continue for the foreseeable future. Here no assumptions can be made, communication between business partners has to be close and continuous.

Notification of change

Specifically, the terms of trade and pricing are agreed formally to ensure that all interests are met. There is provision for any proposed changes, on either side, to be implemented only after suitable consultation. Similarly, new in-market conditions are reviewed jointly: a supplier might be able to offer an extra discount to meet a higher sales tax, a product or service modified or enhanced to meet new regulations or competitive challenge.

Given reasonable communication links, each party can draw upon a joint pool of experience: the supplier will have information on how similar situations have been handled elsewhere; the agent or local office will know how matters have been arranged by competitors in the market.

Partners' financial strength

Suppliers are wise, particularly in times of rapid change, to maintain one other communication link: an independent monitor of the health and status of the agent or associate, no matter how well-established or long the relationship. Possibly there is in the agreement provision for the supply of the audited accounts and balance sheet. If not, other sources of intelligence, such as specialist agencies or the banks, are used to ensure that in one way or the other, the communication network obtains independent information regularly on the financial situation of business partners.

Results against budget

Sales and new contracts are reported regularly, in standard format as set down in the policy manual. Information on sales is usually required quickly – if only as input to production planning – and a statistical return without comment can be completed and transmitted with the minimum of delay.

To be relevant, comment on the results involves the time of senior branch or agency management, and if not available on call, can seriously delay the reporting. Normally, comment and opinion form part of the separate management report.

The basic sales return is not confined to the 'raw' data of turnover during the period. The format sets the results against comparative data – the figures achieved in the previous period, the year-to-date, the current quarter, last year. Of prime importance are the comparisons with budget and the reforecasts, i.e. what it is hoped to achieve in the light of the developing situation. However, to avoid confusion, the basis of all calculations, particularly for the charting of graphs and trends, has to be agreed and understood by all involved in preparing and using the data. These definitions are perhaps best set out in the professional accountancy standards handbook.

Where applicable, the returns also carry stock figures – goods on order, in transit, held locally, set against average and current sales statistics. The return will then automatically show the items and quantities that should now be ordered – in sum, providing a primary communication link between the field and production planning, marketing analysis, finance and general management.

The market management report

The market reports from local management are more subjective than the statistical data but are also submitted to a deadline and set out in an agreed format. Preparation of such material can appear to be a bureaucratic burden for busy people but much of the value lies in this very stipulation of regularity and standardization.

The obvious purpose of the market report is to keep the supplier or head office informed of the current market situation, of competitive activity, environmental developments. Less obvious is the benefit of the report to the compiler – but it is a plus to have to sit down regularly, perhaps once a month, and to think through all elements of a situation. It proves to be a valuable exercise for the manager and his team – and incidentally, helpful to the development of communication skills.

Sales analysis

The first section of a market report will usually comment on the period's results, particularly in comparative terms, setting the figures against equivalent periods, budget and re-forecast. The impact of special situations, perhaps the results achieved with new products or services, the signing of new contracts and customers, and trends and prospects, are all featured.

Marketing programme

The marketing section of the report records progress with the current programme, detailing steps being taken for making up shortfalls or further exploiting areas of success. Much of a marketing plan is fixed for any given period in terms of the message, media mix, sales effort and support but there is usually some room to manoeuvre – by a change of emphasis, by adjustment to the discount structure or by switch of sales effort.

Such decisions may be within the competence of local management and simply noted for possible comment, or the report is the communication channel for making proposals. Change might be sought in pricing or discounting, with special arrangements or the advertising schedule or any element of the complex marketing mix.

The nature of the business governs the marketing areas that will receive detailed attention in the Management Report. A computer software house will watch the machine time capacity and availability. The country manager for a pharmaceutical company will probably receive supplies from a central factory and have but little interest in manufacturing capacity – but his or her report will have a section devoted to the local health care administration, noting latest proposals to control social security costs and drug prices.

The customer

The client or customer section, an important element of the management report, will highlight product and service-performance complaints, comments and suggestions. While not always given attention by local management, this section is a fruitful source of intelligence for enhancement and the development of new ideas. A point considered of little import at in-market level may, if noted and communicated, be recognized as significant and important at head office, where the data are built into the global picture.

For a business working with a limited number or even with individual clients, this section is of prime importance: a reaction, whether favourable or adverse, in one market or area can affect relations and alter opportunities elsewhere, even on a world basis. Recording unfavourable points does require a disciplined approach but is encouraged given recognition of the overall value to the enterprise of sound communication. Reports exist to notify and analyse problems and difficulties and not simply to record success and achievement.

The environment

A communication handicap is that business managers are not journalists with a sense of 'news' and are not necessarily able to recognize and then record what may appear at local level to be mundane matters – but are in fact evidence of important change. Often, too, a competitor's new idea or activity is under-valued or dismissed as misguided and not fully communicated – until it is too late to prevent serious impact.

The environment, including legal and regulatory proposals, is a difficult area to cover in the management report. Developments are rarely instantaneous and universal and with the passage of time, a market manager can lose sight of the significance to the company as a whole of what is happening locally. On the other hand, there is the temptation to note and discuss broad political and economic matters which in fact feature in the world press and are generally known. The general background can be quoted as responsible for shortfalls and disappointments, perhaps as the excuse for inaction.

To have the market report devoted to the relevant and the current is a function of both training and of full downward communication.

Technology and innovation

A section of the report notes and comments on technology and change seen in the marketplace. Innovation can produce spectacular change. In Britain, the established insurers, although world leaders in their field, failed to grasp and then exploit the potential of the computer for targeting sales by market segmentation. They have been overtaken by an entrepreneur, Peter Wood, who founded Direct Line to sell insurance-by-telephone to the computer-defined cream of the motor market.

Not even the most established of leaders can afford to be complacent, to cease continual monitoring of the 'areas of the unknown'. An oft-quoted, classic example occurred in the 1950s when the traditional razor was swept aside virtually overnight by the strip blade. Gillette, the dominant manufacturer, who had ignored the development, lost the lead position for a decade, worldwide.

Development is rarely that drastic and, given market monitoring, adaptation can be planned. Who now makes a slide ruler, a mechanical calculator? Established manufacturers in the booming 1960s had a long lead-in period to adapt and embrace the new electronic technology. Many were not sufficiently in touch or did not have the ability to absorb and use the information that came to hand, and were quick to disappear. Household names of the time, such as Facit and Gross, leading manufacturers of mechanical calculators and cash registers, have been forgotten. Others, such as Olivetti and NCR, linked to their markets, went on and exploited the new opportunities.

An effective communications network gives alert management the lead time for considered decision, even if the conclusion is to dispose of assets while these still have value. Going out of business voluntarily in the face of changing conditions is a sore nettle to grasp but it is a valid choice when compared to soldiering on into bankruptcy.

The norm is not revolution but gradual – and continuous – change, which the market players can absorb, plan to meet and even to lead. News of potential developments is usually published and known well ahead of any market impact and can be captured well in advance by a functioning network.

Competition

Competitive activity is an important feature of routine reporting but there is a difficulty. Competition being continuous, it can be tedious simply to go on repeating information that changes little from period to period. A useful technique is for the competition to be listed on an attachment with any new or noteworthy developments added by way of flagged insertions. Such updating is simple on any electronic system and a standard layout ensures that review of competitive activity is continuous.

Objectivity is the aim but it is easy for a manager to note the favourable and rationalize the negative. There is strong temptation to under-estimate the competition and to anticipate success through personal sagacity. New and (even more so) failing competition might well attract comment and attention while the activities of a traditional competitor, possibly one of greater significance, will be thought so familiar as not to be worth mentioning. It is one function of the central desk to update head office records and to query apparent gaps in reporting.

Staffing and personnel

It can be held that staffing and personnel affairs are too sensitive for inclusion in routine reporting but as people are the key component of any activity, people 'events' and important developments are to be noted. Topics include the adequacy of staffing levels, the availability of technical skills, training programmes (always worth a dedicated section in a structured report), legal developments and trade union activity.

It is also necessary to record individual events, the resignation of a key employee or the recruitment of an exceptional person. Perhaps there has been a notable success – a local team has overcome a difficulty – and those involved deserve special recognition direct from the president.

The regular review of staff for the purpose of reporting is of value to a manager. An enforced pause for thinking on the health of the 'people relationship' in the unit can well pre-empt problems as well as suggest improvements.

ENSURING RESPONSE AND FEEDBACK

Maintaining communication requires discipline but in fact any system works best when seen to be useful to both sides, without being unduly burdensome to either. Given a format and training, the routine of regular reporting should take but little time – a systematic manager will keep running notes and will then only need to pause briefly to compile his report.

The quid pro quo is useful feedback, illustrative of the use to which the material is being put and of its value. Feedback includes individual letters of acknowledgement and comment, review at periodic face-to-face meetings and the circulation of summaries by mail or via on-line terminal.

One other benefit of standard and routine reporting lies in the value of historical material: a browse through a market report file can be the first step of a planning cycle, providing a useful introduction to a market for a visitor or a new employee.

Checking and updating

Communication links with head office require periodic review to ensure that formats are still relevant and continue to be timely. A system of flash estimates might be called for, perhaps for the introduction of new products, or management may require a monitor of areas of potential new business.

There is always some difficulty in maintaining a reporting structure, even when backed by an efficient central desk. It helps for the policy manual pro-formas to emphasize brevity and relevance. If there is nothing to report for a period, then a standard section can be left blank – but not dropped (when it has a tendency to disappear permanently).

The pro-formas also make clear that generalized 'background' discussion – comment on politics or the economic situation – is not required unless matters directly impact on operations. Field and in-market personnel are understandably tempted to 'educate' head office on local affairs but reports must concentrate on what is relevant to the corporation's activities. This can be made plain in direct terms – by returning an edited report to a loquacious executive.

MAINTAINING THE ANNUAL CYCLE

Planning and budgeting

Much of routine communication flows through and from the annual round of meetings and conferences. Typically the cycle starts with long-range planning sessions within each unit and geographic area, leading into the budget meetings and the final presentations seeking approval from executive management or the board.

Throughout the cycle, managers are presenting plans, discussing ideas, making suggestions to their peers, a vital part of company-wide communication. At the end of the process drafts and verbal discussion turn into the formal budget document that launches next year's programme.

In a company-wide communication environment, every employee, starting with those on the shopfloor or on the front desk, is involved in the planning process and given the opportunity to contribute. In turn, all are informed of the results – the objectives and plans for the individual unit – and are also shown its place in the overall scheme, the corporation's global vision.

During the year much of management effort is devoted to the regular review of current status against budget but it is rare for any update information to be communicated down the line. Not everything can or need be published but given a company-wide network the broad outlines of how matters stand are made known. Communication cannot be effective if the workforce never has any idea of progress and sees no results.

Meetings and conferences

Meetings are a continuous feature of management life, a broad definition perhaps being that any gathering of over 20 is best considered and handled as a conference.

Given company-wide communication, there will be a framework, a 'culture' and perhaps broad guidelines set down in the policy manual, for these occasions. Regular meetings may well follow a routine but occasional or special events require thought and preparation on the part of the convenor. The purpose and suggested agenda are circulated in advance and finalized as contributions are agreed with the active participants. The accepted procedures might well provide that events start on time, no matter who is missing, agendas and all materials are available in advance and, most important, that the preparation of minutes is a requirement.

Copy of the record is routinely sent to the central desk both for networking potential not obvious to the participants and for possible contribution to line communication.

Meetings and conferences are a primary channel of communication with the marketplace and the outside world. The annual general meeting with shareholders is obviously given great care as are discussions with financial analysts and the banks. A parallel effort is required in-house. An example would be the annual report, often only casually available to employees but in fact offering a great opportunity for in-house communication. These results can be the occasion for top management making direct contact with the staff through a round of presentations and meetings at all important locations.

Communication at industry fairs and conventions includes contact with suppliers, parallel interests and competitors – generally keeping in touch with the environment. There can be a tendency to regard a regular event as something of a jamboree, to be enjoyed and then forgotten except as a source of folklore.

Conferences are expensive occasions and the results need to be fully exploited and not necessarily by the attendees alone. A simple communication network technique is to have **attendance reports** produced as a matter of routine. These will, for instance, note the theme and display of each competing participant, the thrust of presentations, summarize papers and review technological developments. An attendance report can include a 'gossip' section – the news on competitors, on the moves of prominent personalities – picked up in conversations and these items can be as important as the formal material.

Attendance reports are not a common requirement but can prove invaluable to product managers, the advertising agency and research and development. Also useful is the publication of a synopsis in the company magazine, ensuring that colleagues, perhaps with an unsuspected interest, are alerted and can request further details.

Visiting and visitors

Visits are a key communication link, from 'showing the flag' trips by senior managers to routine financial audit or specialist consultations. Again, much of the value in visiting lies in preparation.

A visitor arranges adequate prior briefing, is careful with the agenda and agrees a timetable that suits the host. In turn, the office prepares the necessary materials and data, makes appointments and ensures that the relevant people will be available.

These are all obvious points – and yet very often honoured in the breach. Much of the frustration of travelling and visiting comes from ignoring the obvious and failure to plan. A checklist governing visits, from identification of purpose, through authorization arrangements, can, for instance, feature in the policy manual. It will be a simple document but its very existence will help avoid what can be expensive waste and loss.

Either visitor or host prepares the **visit report** which, as with meeting and attendance records, is circulated not only to the immediate participants but also to colleagues with a potential interest. Some events are also of sufficient interest to be communicated down the line by the central desk or noted in the internal newsletters.

KEEPING THE NETWORK TECHNICALLY UP-TO-DATE

Effective communication is primarily a function of human motivation but this is much encouraged and made easier by the availability of adequate facilities. An efficient network recognizes that office technology becomes ever more friendly, both in terms of use and by providing links over time and space,

The mushrooming of home-based enterprise apart, significant proportions of the employed population are working remotely and for longer periods of time. These individual 'virtual' offices allow staff to be placed directly into each area of the market.

Alternatively, a modest central location provides the base for an employee force much larger than could be accommodated in a traditional office. A staff of executive or 'empowered' secretaries arranges the schedules of activity, handles messages, makes contacts, notifies queries via the fax or electronically. Outgoing mail is also handled in the same manner, passed between screens, and even confidential data is transmitted behind protective codes.

The management of the communication network has two imperatives:

1. **Technical** – Technology is moving with bewildering speed but it does much for morale, the general environment, to be seen to be keeping up with the market. Apart from computers and updated software, there needs to be ready access to copying and desktop publishing equipment, to quality printers and presentation material production, perhaps to video-conferencing facilities. These tools require some form of technical back-up, whether employed direct or guaranteed by suppliers; equipment failure is simply not acceptable.

   The routine of operations apart, the electronic messaging systems allow two-way contact between management and every employee and can be extended to customers and suppliers. At the same time, the very accessibility of the means of contact can lead to workers, managers and customers being swamped with data, requests, proposals and for the systems to be misused by the disaffected and the mischievous. Handling these situations and foreseeing the potential difficulties is another strong argument for a senior manager to be dedicated to communication.

2. **Human** – There is still no substitute for face-to-face contact. Voice liaison with 'the office', even when fixed and regular, is not enough. Without periodic direct contact, the development of invisible barriers to full communication is inevitable, misunderstandings will arise, leading to demotivation and even resentment. People have to meet, sit down and talk directly to each other in order first, to establish a link and subsequently to ensure that they continue to understand each other.

Bill Gates, the founder of Microsoft, the leading software supplier, puts the point this way: 'E-Mail is not a good way to get mad at someone since you can't interact. You can send friendly messages very easily since they are harder to misinterpret.'

The director responsible for communication does well to ensure that it is part of the established routine, of the normal cycle of activity, for every individual to have direct contact or forms part of a group which meets, sits down to talk and listen. A team is built in no other way.

The Communication Health Index

With all arrangements in place, procedures understood and operational, it is still necessary to ensure that changing needs continue to be met and that the network is as functional as possible. Operational experience will lead to adjustment and adaptation but regular, overall assessment by the compilation of a Communication Health Index is necessary to ensure that the fundamental structure is sound (Chapter 11).

SUMMARY

Company-wide communication is built upon its recognition as a function, to be built and managed by a senior director.

Much of the network is dependent on routines which ensure the two-way flow of data, both between the external world and the corporation and internally, linking everyone in the organization. The emphasis is on the **4C Principle of Communication**: it must be clear, continuous, complete and current.

The relevant definitions, requirements and procedures are established throughout the organization, a published policy manual being the most suitable vehicle for the purpose.

The network stays abreast of advancing technology but also ensures, and places emphasis on every individual being kept in personal contact with colleagues and management.

Periodic review through the Communication Health Index ensures that the network is being maintained and that response and feedback is seen as being satisfactory and informative.

4

LINKING PEOPLE INTO COMPANY-WIDE COMMUNICATION

Linkage to the communication network is a powerful motivation for individuals to identify both with the organization and corporate objectives. The directors must give the business a clear focus and then communicate and put in place the programmes that will develop and continue to train people to meet these aims.

INTRODUCTION

The aim of company-wide communication is to link each individual into the network and, in doing so, to harness all the available talent, effectively and continously, to meeting the corporate objectives. Given the will and a sense of direction, every organization has it within its grasp to build a motivated and dedicated team.

Experience in the real world

A biography of Jack Welch, the chairman of General Electric and arguably the outstanding US business leader of his age, notes that in addition to the publicized restructuring of the corporation, there has been a transformation more subtle but of greater long-term importance:

> Welch has been trying to create an organization which embraces change as inevitable, rather than resisting it; where information

flows freely around the group, rather than being jealously hoarded; and where employees are given important powers to control their working environment.[1]

Change was, is and will be continuous but the temptation is not to notice, to remain static, for effort and thinking to concentrate on the routine and the current. Ironically, communication itself can contribute to paralysis. The expansion of knowledge, paralleled by the faster availability of data of ever-increasing scope, is a challenge and can appear as a looming threat. One reaction is to ignore the news – it may never happen. Another is to devote disproportionate energy and time to keeping abreast of events, to becoming over-analytical – to lose sight of the ball in studying the playing field.

The evidence is clear and fills the financial pages every day: the life-cycle of any business that does not adapt is shortening. Even a cursory backward glance will recall names once known in every household and since lost to sight, forgotten within a decade. Management knows that it is vital to stay informed, to be aware of change, but it is not difficult to become confused, to feel lost.

For an organization to stay on track and to remain focused, there has to be a vision of purpose and function, a grand strategy and a staff that is fully involved and motivated by continuous communication.

The difficulties in the way of maintaining all-round contact have been well illustrated by Sir Denys Henderson, the chairman of ICI, when he reviewed the momentous demerger of pharmaceuticals from the traditional business. The process began or was accelerated by a potential hostile bid for the entire company. In the event of a fight, the attitudes of financial markets, of shareholders and of senior managers would have been crucial.

Sir Denys recalls: 'We had the naive belief that in the heart of every fund manager was a little bit labelled ICI.' In fact, he found that the financial institutions showed indifference, even hostility in the face of the company's record. Equally salutary was the reaction of senior management. 'They clearly did not wish to have Hanson (the potential predator) come in, but equally they were less convinced about the cohesion of ICI and the synergy across the group than we had imagined.'

On reflection, Sir Denys believes that attitudes developed in the sellers' markets of earlier decades lingered on, resulting in divisional executives not identifying either with the overall corporate objectives or with outside interests and the shareholders. In effect, the lack of a communication network, even one linking senior management, brought this corporation to a crisis point where its very existence was threatened.

THE ROLE OF THE DIRECTORS

The directors carry the obvious responsibilities of defining and updating the purpose of the business, its current positioning and where it is aiming to go. Jack Welch, for instance, ruled that any General Electric business not first or second in its sector had to go – and then went ahead and sold companies by the score. Many were doing well, perhaps continued to do so, but a focused GE has continued to grow while other giants – such as General Motors, IBM and Kodak – have been traumatized.

More immediately, directors set annual targets sufficient to provide a return for existing shareholders and to meet development needs. Communication starts at this point, with the directors having to ensure the acceptance and understanding of their requirements by the executive teams responsible for meeting the targets. In the process, the implications for the future of the enterprise, for employment and individual prospects, will all be considered. Also to be reviewed is the impact of operations, of methods of doing business, on the general well-being and on the environment.

Overall, directors carry a heavy communication burden. Their first joint task is to ensure the full publication of plans and aims and then, individually, to listen to reactions. At meetings and presentations, directors have then to reply to comment and to amplify and explain the corporate position. Unfortunately it is not common practice and in fact, directors and senior executives rarely accept their full role as internal communicators.

While contact is maintained, in some degree at least, with the outside world, with the shareholders and other financial interests, when did the managing director or chief executive last make a presentation to the workforce? The ritual 'thank you' note to the staff in the annual report does not communicate well to anyone. In general, business leaders have much to learn from politicians in meeting their 'public'.

Directors and the planning process

A former chairman of ICI, Sir Maurice Hodgson, has described how the planning process was activated at this giant British chemical concern. When he was given the portfolio earlier in his career, planning was 'out there' somewhere, the responsibility of a dormant board sub-committee.

Sir Maurice, as he subsequently became, started by posing a simple question:

> Where are we now – where do we want to be – how do we propose to get there?

Here was a striking application of the **4C** Communication Principle: the question, clearly defining the current concern, was complete in itself and yet raised a concern of continuing relevance.

Of course, the answers are never complete: the passing of each year makes necessary the renewed consideration of the question. In this way the planning cycle is restarted afresh.

Defining the business – the 'where are we now?' – is never as straightforward as it would appear from the simplicity of the question. The first reaction from the board of ICI might well have been, 'We're in the chemicals business' – but this answer immediately leads on to such further detail as:

- Which chemicals? Do we stay with the base chemicals or do we aim to produce the end-products, e.g. pharmaceuticals?
- Is our management capable of handling such a business?
- Is our technology up-to-date and ahead of competition? Are the research facilities adequate?
- Where in geographic terms are we situated and where are our customers? Our potential?

Each stage and series of questions helps to clarify the 'where do we want to be?' and then identifies the actions necessary to reaching the desired point, achieving the directors' objectives. ICI was put on the track of continued growth and prosperity for another generation, until the process of change was allowed to falter and communication with the market became obscured.

Similar debate is involved in the positioning of services, a consultancy, a publisher and provider of data or information or a finance house. The question remains: 'Exactly what is the market and then, the segment in which we operate? Is this a stable/growing/declining area and, no matter what that status, is technology impacting the scope and availability of what is currently on offer now/in the immediate future/in the longer term?'

The focus of any organization – be it a charity or an executive agency of government – is equally subject to continuous change; the Red Cross of today has little resemblance to the bands of volunteers who attended to the abandoned wounded on the battlefields of nine-teenth-century Europe.

The effectiveness of communication is key to the success of the planning cycle during which these questions are posed each year. The network carries the updated intelligence on the resources available and on the market, the basis on which the operating plan is refocused. The corporation sets a course to meet identified change and the pattern of people involvement falls into place.

Figure 4.1 shows the links between people in the planning and implementation processes of an organization.

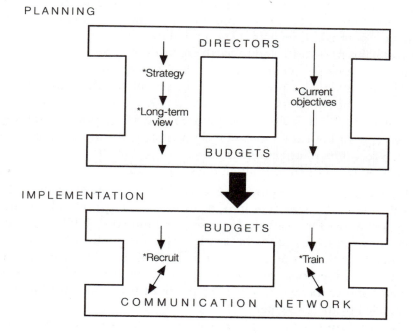

Figure 4.1 The people links.

THE DEVELOPMENT OF PEOPLE

Recruitment: a two-sided process

Successful recruitment is a function of communication. Initially there is advertising in the open market and the preparation of materials for use in the universities and colleges. Subsequently comes the individual contact, when the process of selection must also convey the right impression of the enterprise to the applicants.

The jargon which features even in professional recruitment advertising conveys a poor image of thoughtlessness, if not uncertainty. Specification of requirements for the 'talented', 'truly visionary', 'highly motivated' communicates nothing so much as lack of clear objectives. What is to be made of employers who describe themselves as 'dynamic' in contrast to those seeking 'dynamic' recruits? It is discouraging to find demands for skill and experience in age groups that could not possibly have acquired them.

Recruitment must keep one eye on the standpoint of the potential applicants, those whom it is sought to attract. Each generation has its attitudes, a change of approach and it is the employer who must adapt. Staying in touch, maintaining a communication link with social change helps to smooth, and to sooth the process.

Top positions are often filled on a person-to-person basis through headhunting. Perhaps not the most popular of people with 'victim' companies, headhunters succeed in a tough environment by being careful with definition and specification. Each situation is carefully analysed from both sides, an approach that can usefully be applied to general recruitment programmes.

Planned recruitment is built on the **4C** principle:

- **Continuity** – the employer has a recruitment strategy. At the individual level this translates into identifying career paths and offering opportunities for creativity, leadership and initiative. While the civilian environment cannot be as clear-cut, the professional Army's officer recruitment programme has useful lessons. In particular, the cadet is offered opportunities to show his or her mettle on every count and at the end is left in no doubt of his or her suitability as revealed by the assessment.
- **Completeness** – the employer has a concrete business plan, pointing the individual to specific projects, products and services.
- The programme is **clear** both in the documentation and during the face-to-face employment process.

- The employer, pointing to achievements in the sector, demonstrates awareness of **current** trends and the ability to stay at the forefront of events. In turn the recruit understands that he or she will be given the training opportunities and will be expected to update professional and other skills continually.

A programme for integration

The recruit is linked into the communication network from the start. One useful method, wherever feasible, is to give the newcomer overall exposure to the customer, the suppliers and appropriate departments. Given company-wide communication, stress is laid on the obvious during the process – that there is communication into and out of every position.

In this environment the recruit is not exposed to the common perception of poor communication but is made conscious of each worker's responsibility for the input of data to others, no matter how routine. The network is seen as an element of every function, that it is not simply an ad hoc system for the distribution of working instruction and the collection of necessary operational data.

Involvement through consultation

First personal entry into the network can be to join in the consultation process.

Company-wide communication offers every worker a direct channel for the transmission of ideas and suggestions through some form of quality control circle. The process is well-established at industrial plants but is also applicable to office and clerical staff. They too have problems and can see ways of improving the efficiency of daily routine. Here the recruit will experience positive attitudes to the work in hand and will perhaps see that recommending change elsewhere, in another's work pattern, does also lead to a realistic assessment of one's own efforts.

Imaginative use of new employees' introductory period is an integral element of the recruitment process – and of the management of company-wide communication.

THE ROUTINE OF COMMUNICATION

The personal link of consultation

While the communication network is multi-faceted, the most personal link for the majority is the consultation process through which every employee has operational contact with management.

Many companies are proud to exceed the legal benefit requirements in such areas as pensions, the various leave and holiday entitlements, sickness provisions and the like. It is equally important however, to make people feel they are part of the team. The consultation process is key to what in Germany is known as the *betriebsklima*, the working climate. Companies are very conscious of this 'climate' as is evident from the emphasis placed upon it in employment advertising.

The 'climate' is reflected tangibly – in absenteeism, sickness, staff turnover rates and in the attitude of managers to each other: willing cooperation or obstruction. Consultation is necessarily tailored, ranging from quality control circles to self-managing teams, from works councils to project groups. Whatever the system, the key feature is for the individual to feel involved, to be able to contribute and, importantly, to be recognized for the contribution.

In the company-wide communication environment, the consultation process is two-way – up the line with suggestions, ideas, even comments and queries; in return, clear response from management, acknowledgement and, again most importantly, discussion of plans and objectives. Nothing short of catastrophe should come as a surprise.

Consultation is not limited to the specific, possibly technical area but set into the overall framework of investment, impact on profitability – even, as may well be the case, the implications for employment. The concept can be uncomfortable but communication implies trust. The people trusted with the manufacture of the product, the delivery of the service, where mistakes can be disastrous, are also to be trusted with the plans and results on which their livelihoods depend. Equally, their views are to be seen to be sought on the possible impact of developments, technological changes or events likely to impinge on existing systems and operations.

Failure to do so divorces even the enlightened employer from the workforce, unfortunate at the best of times but a disaster in a crisis. This was the position in which Birds Eye Walls, a British subsidiary of the Unilver world food corporation, found itself when it decided to close an ice cream business. The unit was profitable in itself but judged not to warrant the investment necessary to bring it up to world standards. The decision raised a storm in the affected community and soon involved both British and European Union politicians.

The shutdown was finally averted by a management buyout but not before the loss of much goodwill (not only locally) and at the cost of much management time. Obvious throughout the controversy was the complete divide between owner and worker. It was summed up by one quote in the national press: ' I didn't even know I was part of Walls till they tried to kick us into touch.'

Open access to data

Change of attitudes does not come overnight but, on close examination, much of the assumed need for confidentiality lies in the mind of management. Nevertheless, the trend is towards more access by investors, workers or outside interests to hitherto concealed data. In fact, openness has proved a spur to effort as companies are increasingly forced to view results in the light of competitive achievement.

An example lies in the more open accounting of the banks, first in Britain and now gradually elsewhere in Europe. The change has caused none of the difficulties once feared – there have been no run on funds in times of crisis – but has seen an explosion of competitive services and facilities.

At the same time, it has to be recognized that what a workforce can perceive as secrecy might be no such thing. The ubiquitous 'they' are always up to something but in fact for a given period there may only be the routine with nothing to say. At such times, however, it may be as well to keep the mechanism of consultation functioning, if only to prevent suspicion that the untoward is 'cooking'.

The visit and exchange programme

By definition, organization involves a structure. Marketing functions apart from the sales force and the factory or computer centre may well be remote from either. People in different areas of the corporation might have no contact with each other, and little concept of how others live and work.

Company-wide communication seeks to maximize people synergy through direct contact. Points of potentially useful contact are identified by the director overseeing communication, possibly in part through the consultative set-up, and a visit programme is developed in the business plan for the year. For instance, there is usually mutual benefit from having the freight and shipping people visit the various production facilities; for the front office to meet the computer technicians.

This programme is quite apart from the normal routine of visits and meetings – it is designed to bring workforce people together. Initially, these occasions will be exploratory, quite possibly direct benefit might be hard to identify for a time. In the end, the value of this level of contact has to be determined by those involved, through the consultative process. Some elements might well be dropped, for a time at least, but certainly others will continue and even expand.

Much will depend on the careful preparation of agendas – and the degree of commitment that the communication approach has built.

Communicating the operational plan

Planning and the consequential setting of budgets is an exercise that absorbs much of management time. Once approved, each operation's plan is neatly bound and implementation begins.

While past achievement and results are widely broadcast, public discussion of the future has to be more restrained, but the fact that employees' interest lies in the way ahead should not be overlooked. Last year's pay has been banked and spent and it is future prospects that are of concern – enhanced earnings, the role and place in the scheme of things for the individual. Too often, the staff, told on the one hand of the gratitude of management, are then denied a view of what lies ahead. There appears to be no confidence in the workforce – or management gives the impression of believing that the employees can be ignored.

Even when plans for a large investment, a technological success, a special contract are announced, it is with one eye on the authorities and the other on the financial markets. The interest of the workforce in these matters can be lost to sight – when in fact it should at the very least be given equal weight.

The two-way process of data flow

Communication and the trust on which it is built is a two-way process: a management that fails to take the employees into its confidence cannot expect loyalty and trust to develop spontaneously. To summarize the annual plan, the campaigns and developments and the areas of change, is not a major task. A clear and concise report to the staff sets the tone and spirit for the year ahead.

Publication of the plan can be via the terminals, in the magazines or perhaps by special enclosure with each pay slip. More effectively, each manager presents the plan to the staff, in this way completing the communication circle from the consultative groups, through the planning process back to the employees.

With working units becoming smaller and peripheral tasks, from running the canteen to managing laboratories, being contracted out, the planning process starts at lower levels. Major industries, with Japanese car manufacturers being a prime example, arrange for all components to be supplied by an integrated network of small, specialist producers.

In the exploration for, and exploitation of oil, virtually every function may be contracted out, from the early geological surveys to the running of the canteen in an established field. Leading retail chains everywhere contract out for the supply of their lines, using independent design teams, dedicated factories.

The web becomes complex but the trend has the advantage that more people become fully involved in their work, not simply as operatives but in the overall planning and execution process. In turn, they feel a need for a view of the 'big picture', the state of the whole organization or sector: to understand how the jigsaw fits together.

Today's workers are also sophisticated – every living room, whether that of the clerk or the director, has the same 'electronic windows' open to the world. People travel, possibly read more widely and many continue to study. These are all factors that lead to heightened expectations of interest in and satisfaction from work.

In this environment, a management that bemoans lowered interest in their tasks by workers, less dedication and the disappearance of 'traditional' loyalties, perhaps unwillingness to take on new tasks and change skills, must take a long, hard look at itself and its communications.

TRAINING FOR COMMUNICATION

Business training in the main concentrates on improving management and financial capabilities – an understanding of the role of communication is simply assumed.

Japanese corporations work differently and integrate communication from the start with their team approach to operations. It is as a team that data is gathered, analysed and discussed and that a decision is reached. The system implies sharing responsibility – and, in turn, joint recognition and satisfaction. The subtlety is that by definition a team is a live and vibrant unit of communication. Every member of the group has to be informed and take part, as do related specialist teams and higher management: all ask questions and look for more data throughout the process.

The basis is the development and communication of a strategic plan for training. This sets out to:

- provide the skills needed for meeting the laid-down, published objectives; as these change and advance with each planning period, so training is recognized as being a continuous process;
- encourage individuals to recognize that enhancement of skills opens up new opportunities;
- offer everyone, from the shopfloor upwards, the opportunity of further training. If every French soldier carries a marshal's baton in his kit, every worker can measure him- or herself for the executive chair and, in the meantime, feel they 'belong'.

The trend towards empowerment and re-engineering is breaking down the traditional manager–worker relationship. Where the hierarchy is replaced by teams dedicated to core processes or handling specific tasks, managers take on a more enabling role in providing information, checking performance, recording results. Communication is central to the process, within the teams, between functions and in keeping the focus on the overall budget objectives. In the new environment, training in communication is an imperative.

Individual responsibility is more the norm in the West but acceptance of the company-wide communication concept does not call for dramatic change, the introduction of new systems and methods. Existing resources are harnessed – and training is a key element of the process.

Communication training of senior management

Communication training for senior management is often offered for the development of a personal skill, in the delivery of presentations or public speaking. More generally, top managers may study the handling of public relations, contact with trade unions and organized labour or the implementation of legal requirements.

The concept of studying communication as a function is novel. The first step is to gain an insight into shortcomings, the perceived needs of the organization as revealed by internal polls, the consultative groups or brought to light by consultants. Often revealed is a gap in a basic skill, usually the inability to recognize what is 'news' and in consequence, a lack of editorial policy, no guidelines for what is to be communicated and how it is to be done. Some of the media of communication may be poorly used or ignored altogether.

Once the opportunities for improvement have been identified, the director handling communication has the difficult task of interesting colleagues in upgrading their participation in the function. The task can be handled by having an established, respected consultant tailor a forum to the profile of the corporation. This involves a degree of trust in the use of company data but at senior level a session dealing with 'real' material has an impact that cannot be achieved with theoretical models.

Full involvement at senior level

The effectiveness of the company-wide communication concept is dependent on the internal climate and stems from the full involvement of the senior executives. They, too, have a need to be refreshed and to accept a programme that has their thinking and the accepted methods re-examined on a regular basis.

Senior executives subject to great change include those in the public sector, where whole areas of administration are switching to the 'accountability' concept, responsible for 'sales' and budgets. Policy-making is separated from operational management so that, for example, a city or health service head is expected to be a chief executive running what in commercial terms can be a very substantial business. Successful operation now calls for personal leadership as much as the old rule-by-the-book methods.

The changes have led to calls for enhanced training at every stage but particularly for courses to help managers adapt and to refresh established executives facing the new challenges. There is no equivalent in the business world to the top executive programmes run by the Civil Service College in Britain but they are a useful guide to what can be developed for a corporate management team.

Middle and operational management

At the middle and operational levels of management, communication training consists of two elements.

First is the tangible. Managers need to know how to handle the routine reporting, the consultation and suggestions procedure. Then there are other elements of the network, the terminals, the notice-board, the magazine, the personnel department, with which it is necessary to be familiar.

In part, 'training' will be an integral element of the routine of contact and meetings – communication as a standing item on the agenda. Understanding of the function is then further enhanced by input from outside professionals on specific topics – hints on running a group discussion, on a recognition and reward structure, on motivation and on the review of market research data. The list can be formidable but if aligned to expressed needs, or identified shortcomings, 'courses' are anticipated events and will be planned into the working routine.

Second, understanding of communication is enhanced by a periodic assessment of the input and output of each desk, office and department. Is the function receiving all the information needed and is it arriving on time? In turn, is the information and data sent out comprehensive and timely? In the process, a manager and each of the operatives realizes that company-wide communication is indeed a personal responsibility, with everyone involved and contributing directly.

Specialist groups

Specialist groups, such as laboratories or design teams, work in relative isolation. Personnel can feel – and in fact, can become – remote from central affairs. Communication training for them aims to keep them in touch with events outside their immediate function. Not only are they given the opportunity but there is also an expectation for them to attend appropriate meetings, events and seminars. A research scientist may hear of market reactions that have not appeared in reports when attending a sales conference; in turn, the 'field' personnel learn something of the difficulties in achieving further improvements and gain product insight.

Formal presentations are particularly rewarding in building understanding between teams. The marketing director can present the full campaign picture to research and development, the chief scientist or engineer can explain the development programme to marketing and sales. I myself have had direct experience of presenting market data to laboratory staff and finding that scientists who had been beavering away for years on lines of research knew nothing of the market structure. Presumably management had set the programme in the light of potential returns but the scientists were fascinated to see the picture. There was a strong need-to-know feeling.

The sales force

A trained sales force also has a communication function. Much time and effort is necessarily invested in the enhancement of selling ability. This is a prime communication skill but it is applied more broadly, to develop the sales force into an important link with the market. Sales people learn to monitor the market, to report on products and customer reactions, and perhaps comment on campaign effectiveness.

A prerequisite to effective reporting is to give people a clear sense of identity with the organization as a whole. Most directly for the sales force, this involves exposure to the overall marketing plans and also being kept in touch with the general progress of the company – the updating for everyone implied in company-wide communication.

Equally important is to ensure that the sales people are encouraged in their communication role by acknowledgement and feedback. The prime objective of sales people is to achieve targets on which their income is, in part at least, directly based. There has to be incentive for them to report adequately.

Since people respond to recognition, the communication training programme also clarifies both the system of response to queries and observations and the criteria by which individuals who provide exceptional input are identified and rewarded. Communication training ensures the field staff are used effectively in their wider role and that they are aware that it is a valuable one.

Training facilities

While much of a continuous programme of training is either on-the-job or by way of relatively short courses, a result of the rapidity of change is that the professions are also required to update qualifications.

One method they have developed is the pleasant round of sponsored seminars, conferences and workshops that is such a feature of the world travel scene. Many hundreds can attend – 50 000 and more delegates participate at the major computer events. At a typical gathering, the executive committees will discuss professional concerns and there will be a full programme of workshops, discussions and presentations for the general body of participants. Also there will be specialist suppliers taking advantage of the market opportunity but at the same time broadcasting the latest advances and innovations. These are communication opportunities for everyone.

An enterprise either invests in training or pays premium rates and offers incentives to attract skilled staff from elsewhere, which is possibly a short-term policy as the mobile population tends to move on again. In-house training fosters a sense of involvement which experience shows is an encouragement to workforce stability.

Economic swings enforce cutbacks and programme postponements, the recovery then sees a scramble for available talent, particularly in areas of technological advance. At its broadest, this is a situation beyond the scope of even the largest organization, calling for cooperation and planning by whole industries and the educational establishment. Even then, matters go badly wrong as witness the growing world surplus of doctors that developed from the 1980s onwards. The educational systems had over-estimated the need for medical staff and the result in a decade was the under-employment and even unemployment of expensively-qualified people.

In the same period, computer experience at any level was at a premium. Educational emphasis simply cannot keep pace with such rapidity of change.

The global situation lends weight to the relatively modest internal programmes. These can be more aligned to immediate needs but there is never any guarantee. During the recessions of the current decade leading employers, such as accountancy firms, have found themselves with a large surplus of trainees.

Nevertheless, for operations to keep abreast of change, training of staff has to continue. Most effort will be devoted to formal courses and programmes but not to be overlooked is the secondment of people between markets and across functions, the attachment of market line managers to technical areas and vice versa, R & D staff to marketing, a European manager to the US, etc.

CONCLUSION

Overall, the **4C** Principle of Communication applies to the training function: the programme is to be Clear, seen to be Continuing, with material and content that is Current and Complete for each skill.

Training is seen to be geared to the published objectives. It is subject to annual assessment but, whatever the circumstances, a programme is budgeted – training is not a variable to be eliminated in periods of difficulty.

SUMMARY

Company-wide communication links all available talent into the network. First the directors communicate their objectives and the plans to meet them.

The linking process starts at the recruitment stage. It continues with the planned integration and then the continued involvement of every individual.

A commitment to continuous training, at every level, includes the development of communication skills.

REFERENCES

1. Tichy, N. and Sherman, S. (1993) *Control Your Own Destiny or Someone Else Will*, Doubleday, London, UK

5

BUILDING PEOPLE INTO COMMUNICATORS

People generally believe they personally communicate adequately. Nevertheless the function as a whole is found wanting. This chapter points to the fact that most people are not natural communicators and need help to develop the skill.

INTRODUCTION

It would be paradoxical for anyone in business or commerce not to consider themselves adequate, perhaps even good communicators. Some are more comfortable on paper, others find conversation or meetings to be the preferred medium and still others (a minority) come across best with presentations. In general, people believe their communication output meets the requirements of colleagues and the business.

Strange then that the level of communication is so often criticized, felt to be insufficient or incomplete and that at every level:

- on the shopfloor or at the front desk, workers can carry out their specific tasks with little notion of being part of a team, of awareness of the objectives;
- middle management lives in fear of the unknown, of strategic planning and financial moves that can have drastic effects overnight on prospects and careers;
- and top management wonders what time-bombs are out there, concealed until a major explosion rocks the board.

BUILDING POSITIVE COMMUNICATION

In an environment of managed communication, each employee is built to become a communicator, to integrate through the network with the team. The organizational objective is for all communication to be contributory and positive, not merely reactionist to instruction, routine in response.

There are those fortunate to be born with the ability to make themselves understood, to be able to guide and enthuse others. Corporations, however, are run by the 'ordinary' executives, by people who welcome help and need training and who, given only the opportunity to participate, will respond.

Table 5.1 lists those elements primarily initiated either by the company or the individual in building positive communication.

Table 5.1 Building the communicator

| Element | Prime initiator | |
	Company	Individual
'Listening'		★
Career review	★	
Counselling	★	
Appearance		★
Language		★
Presentation	★	★
Telephone		★
Writing		★
Travel	★	★
Training	★	

The discipline of listening

The effective communicator is first a good 'listener'. This is not a passive role, of happily allowing others to 'talk', verbally or on paper (and then perhaps going ahead regardless). The listener makes a positive contribution, questioning and commenting – helping to structure a discussion.

It is an interpersonal skill, among those that are the subject of much written work and many educational courses. Typically, the creative development of personal relationships will at some point address the importance of constructive and positive listening. There will be stress on the need for the listener to clear the mind of preconceived perceptions and feelings in order to absorb what is actually being said. It is necessary to be free to grasp the reasoning, even the emotions, lying behind the speaker's words. Only then, it is taught, is it possible to contribute effectively.

The process is not simple, as observation of even routine verbal exchanges will quickly illustrate.

Much of conversation falls into one of two categories:

- the **educational**, during which the speaker passes on 'information', often of no particular significance to either him- or herself or the listener; such talk ranges from views on the weather to road and travel conditions, children's activities and any news of the day;
- the **declamatory**, the voicing of opinion, usually on topics remote to the speaker or listener. Typical subjects would include the ineptitude of the government, people's inefficiencies and shortcomings, and how to put things right.

Constructive exchange, the expression and then the development of thoughts and ideas, is but a small part of person-to-person contact. It is the element that marks the communicator.

Listening is the corollary of constructive conversation. A speaker who feels his or her words are being discounted, even ignored, is discouraged and antagonized, leaving no room for fruitful contact. A listener who is concentrating, seen to be evaluating what is being said, will in turn find his or her comments given attention and thus a relationship will develop.

Much specialist training and reading is devoted to relationships but the following illustrate some of the principles.

- A good listener will encourage the speaker with feedback – 'Have I got this right, you feel that ...?'; 'Are you saying ...?'
- A listener also seeks to uncover reasoning, emotions – 'You evidently believe strongly in....', giving the speaker an opportunity to unburden him- or herself, perhaps see matters in another light. In any event, given such interest, confidence is developed and the constructive process begins.
- The poor listener will react destructively. Typical is the habit of

interrupting before the speaker has made the point. In this way, the listener is making it clear that he or she is too busy with his own important thoughts to pay much attention. Not only is contact broken but the speaker's data can be lost. Apparent or anticipated understanding of what is about to be said can prove sadly wrong.

Turning poor into 'positive' listening

The poor listening pattern includes repeating points made previously, already dealt with in the conversation, and continuing to defend a position with the old arguments against new thoughts. Sterile declamation – or simply showing impatience – are bad habits more easily acquired than discarded.

Opposition and disagreement are to be expected and an argument may be lost or won but ideally only as the outcome of constructive exchange. In the real world, politics and vested interests will affect decisions but professional management at least strives to arrive at considered solutions, after relevant views have been heard and understood.

'Listening' does not apply to the spoken word alone. For many, it requires discipline to 'listen' fully to a message, to read a report and not to react on a first impression or to procrastinate and call for more data.

Much of the material thumping on to the desk may warrant only a cursory glance, there is a limit to how much matter can be read, to what can be examined, but the communicator has to develop the capacity to handle the paper mountain and to identify the relevant. It seems that this is a skill based more on practice, on learning to concentrate than on specific training. The answer certainly does not lie in late hours or bulging briefcases being trotted home – but in self-discipline and the determination to learn concentration and 'listening'.

For those on the shopfloor, at the front desk, there is a first step: the need for opportunities to listen. These come on the individual being linked into the network. Company-wide communication works fully once all have confidence in the system and feel that it is for them. There is access to data, contact with management and all are in a position to 'listen'.

PASSIVE TO ACTIVE COMMUNICATORS

The communication of work is continuous at every level, not only between executives and managers but throughout the organization. The storeperson and the delivery van driver, the computer operator and the receptionist all receive and transmit working data throughout the day.

A trained storeperson has to keep a record of receipts by time, quantity, item, of shipments and of delivery schedules. There will be returns to complete for damages, short deliveries. To become a communicator, however, the storeperson has to have, or be given a mechanism or channel for recording and reporting unusual problems, and for making such suggestions that come his or her way or occur to them.

The move to positive contribution

The move from routine and passive communication to making a positive contribution requires:

- an atmosphere of **encouragement** in which individuals know that suggestions and ideas are welcomed, will be listened to and given attention;
- a recognized **procedure** or mechanism through which matters can be communicated;
- **incentives** to report and contribute, perhaps a recognition and direct reward system for exceptional ideas and contributions.

It is an inexplicable feature of commercial and industrial training that, while years are spent in acquiring a trade or qualification, no emphasis is given to communication. There is little recognition of the very skill that is basic to the individual fulfilling his or her role in the workplace, at whatever level. The importance of effective communication grows with promotion but here again, it is given little if any overt attention – the ability to communicate as such is simply assumed.

A woman or man skilled in a speciality or with intellectual ability is not necessarily able to communicate. Perhaps this becomes even less the case as the individual is promoted, moved to positions not involving the direct exercise of the trade or profession.

The speed of change, paralleled by growing regulatory requirements, has made updating and qualification enhancement the common practice – but without emphasis on developing the ability to communicate. Doctors will be updated on new treatments – but not on how to achieve heightened empathy with patients; engineers and architects will study new materials and systems, but not how to communicate with the people and communities their work affects.

Training in communication

There are courses and teaching programmes devoted to communication, and their range continues to expand, but review of what is available and of prospectuses and agendas reveals a concentration on specific skills. The teaching covers effective presentations or public speaking, perhaps the control and management of meetings.

However, there is a growing awareness of the overall communication function and of need to help the shy and stumbling, the loud and aggressive, to make their full contribution to the network. The techniques are based on having attendees face their emotions and become aware of how these are seen by and affect others. The start is often a self-rating of such characteristics as 'relevance' and 'clarity' and the ability to develop 'empathy'.

Video recordings are made of discussions and presentations. These are subsequently analysed and the behaviour revealed can then be discussed in psychological terms, of the need, for instance, to recognize the effects of insecurity and anxiety or of a desire for acceptance and admiration.

It is not easy to change characteristics that flow from a person's make-up but perhaps some obvious faults can be corrected. Relationships might be improved by a change of approach, perhaps by taking trouble over small matters, or an effort can made to eschew annoying personal habits. A process of cultural change has begun when such steps are combined with improved 'practical' techniques, in presentation, speaking and writing, and there is a heightened awareness of the whole process of communication.

Empowerment and promotion

There is growing emphasis on empowerment, to passing authority and responsibility to those at the workface (Figure 5.1). The salesperson at the point of customer contact can make a decision, turning to his or her manager more for advice than instruction. In the 're-engineered' environment, a budget for a particular function, or a segment of the market, will be run by a self-managing team.

In the more traditional mode, the successful will move to positions in which much of the time will be spent managing others rather than in practising the skill or profession, the area in which one is most literate.

Whichever the system, those faced with additional responsibilities need a consciousness of the key practical skill, the ability to communicate, if they are to be successful in facing the new challenges. Simply learning on the job is not sufficient.

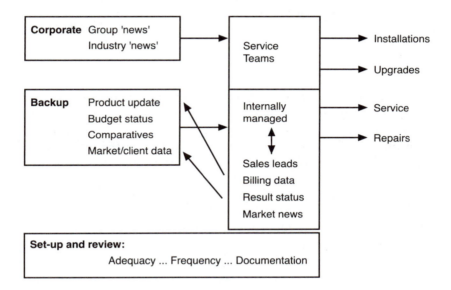

Figure 5.1 Empowerment communication.

Functional teams are by definition units of communication but the practicalities have, nevertheless, to be worked out and accepted by each member. How much time is to be devoted to **planning** and the formal **exchange of data** on progress? What **documentation** is required? How is the two-way flow of intelligence maintained with the corporate network – the market databank, accounting, the specialists, and the supervisory manager or director?

Viewed within the framework of communication, the methods and organization of the teams falls into place. A step-by-step examination of the flow of data to each team, its distribution and absorption – the actual handling of intelligence by the group – and the return flow to the corporate centre, establishes the working environment.

Those promoted outside their area of personal expertise face similar issues, again to be addressed specifically as communication. There is seldom a formal familiarization procedure but the inevitable learning curve is assisted by the new manager and the team assessing the assignment in terms of links with the communication network.

What are the data requirements of the department or section and to what extent are these being met? Is the information being handled to maximum benefit? How well is the department responding to the needs of other elements of the organization? Fulfilling routine data requirements? Posed and answered, these questions set matters on course from the start.

The career review

Even when not recognized as such – and unfortunately that is often the case – communication is central to the annual career review, the written and verbal assessment of progress between an individual and management. The under-achiever who feels isolated or ill-placed might well start by looking at personal communication skills. The supervisor or manager who feels let down by the staff, or who believes the unit's results are not sufficiently appreciated, might also do well to examine day-to-day communication. How is the staff being contacted and motivated? Are the reporting procedures, both in and out, being met? In other words, is he or she fulfilling obligations as fully as others are expected to meet theirs?

Self-assessment and criticism is integral to professional, motivating career reviews. The process starts on a sound basis when communication is recognized as a core skill and the individual's progress and achievement viewed in the light of how well the inward and outward flow of data and intelligence is being handled.

Organization is built by having each level provide effective staff support to those above – the 'followers' function as it is called at the Harvard Business School. However, followers to be useful must exercise critical ability and independence of mind. One authority has pointed out that it is the followers' obligation to share their best thinking with others, the immediate manager: silence is what cannot be accepted. In turn they must find themselves in an environment in which these faculties can be exercised and are welcomed.

The example is quoted of Lee Iacocca, the manager credited with saving the Chrysler car manufacturer, who always had a dissenting 'follower' at every meeting. In this way, he ensured that the other side of the argument was put and heard.

Iacocca, a born communicator, records in his autobiography how he found that at Chrysler if he wanted data to address a problem, 'you had to first put in a system to get the data'. To do that, he worked hard to get the right people – and they had to be able to communicate. Whether it was the witness at Congressional loan hearings or the corporate trade union negotiator or Lee himself, appearing as he did in his own famous advertisements, the theme was:

> The only way you can motivate people is to communicate with them.

A central Iacocca management tool is a **quarterly** review, during which each manager sits with his immediate superior to check accomplishments and chart goals. He writes: 'It sounds almost too simple – except that it works', and goes on to quote the reasons: mutual acceptance of goals, motivation and encouragement to creativity. Also, people don't feel they are buried.

Stress alleviation and counselling

The cost of stress to business and industry, never mind the carry-over effect to private life, is estimated in huge sums by such professional organizations as the British Association for Counselling and the US Employee Assistance Professionals Association. Apart from the cost of stress-induced illness, there are the immeasurable losses resulting from poor judgments and misconceived action.

Linking people into the network helps overcome this major problem of stress. Much anxiety and frustration is removed from the man or woman who can and even has to formulate ideas and knows these will be assessed and appreciated.

Frustration is part of living, matters cannot always be right but in business life it is a great help to be able to communicate the difficulties, ambiguities and perceived 'nonsenses' of the workplace – and to be responded to. Given a system, the employee gains the confidence of being recognized as an individual and in turn feels part of the team and the common effort.

A further response is the provision of professional counselling outside the corporation's own personnel arrangements and management hierarchy. This intense form of person-to-person communication recognizes that private life situations can severely affect output, that the personal and professional interrelate.

Even successful and integrated people can feel the need for professional advice, the 'stranger' with whom it is easier to discuss a marital
or financial problem, than with a close connection. Provision of counselling further communicates the human face of the employer – and
that builds commitment.

BUILDING ON PERSONALITY CHARACTERISTICS

Personal characteristics and behaviour patterns are key elements in the
make-up of the effective communicator. Much working time is devoted
to direct face-to-face or voice contact during which personality builds
the empathy that can decide an issue. Occasionally, reaction on making
a contact is one of 'instant dislike' or of warm sympathy but usually it is
neutral and the relationship develops in the light of experience.

Study of people 'electricity' might one day provide useful insight
into the idiosyncrasies of human behaviour but, meanwhile, first reactions are based on appearance, speech and manners.

Appearance

Appearance is a function of job, fashion and occasion. The grey-
flannel-suit regimes imposed by some corporations in the post-Second
World War period have long since passed away but it is a mistake to do
other than consider appearance in the working environment.

The ethos of the workplace will communicate the day-to-day style
but this may have to be reconsidered for outside contact. Attending a
conference, it may be judged best to be 'one of them', or to be sufficiently different to make an impact. The point is worth a little research
and thought. Appropriate turnout is a politeness and a mark of respect,
a sense of style creates an atmosphere.

Consciously or not, care in appearance communicates a strong
message to an audience or a host. Dress codes continue to exist, if only
to specify neatness and modesty, and there is little to be gained by
needlessly ignoring what is acceptable. The most 'liberated' are
unlikely to welcome judges with nose rings or be comfortable with
having their doctor in a sweat shirt.

Language

Speech and accents are today usually accepted for what they are and it should no longer be a disadvantage to speak with a regional or 'class' accent. However, tone and phraseology still mark the person – sloppy language does not often help to communicate a point to a business gathering.

Personal affection apart, people would appear to communicate best with those sharing their cultural and ethnic background – but common identity does not necessarily equate with understanding. In fact, perceived similarities can lead to assumptions of understanding that in the event prove unfounded. Obvious cultural differences tend to ensure more careful communication.

English has become so universal a medium that it is easy to assume understanding but it has its difficulties, even for the native speaker. James Thurber, the great American comic writer, recalled overhearing as a child in his mother's drawing room the remark that 'old Mrs Huston was terribly cut up after her daughter died on the operating table'. Apparently the young James then spent many a sleepless hour imagining the surgeons dealing with the poor Mrs Huston after they had done with the daughter.

Difficulties of understanding between generations can be compounded in contacts between the many peoples for whom English is now the mother tongue. Words change in meaning and have different connotations in different countries and regions.

Experienced executives are careful of their choice of words at home and abroad but it is helpful if known pitfalls within the corporate or even industry vocabulary are recorded on a central database. The subject is considered in more detail in connection with international communication (Chapter 9) but a corporate thesaurus, and a behavioural profile by country, are not difficult to develop and incorporate into an on-line network. These are links that can prove of great value both to the individual faced with an unknown or new situation and to the corporation in avoiding the repetition of mistakes.

This is part of established familiarization practice for Foreign Office and government employees going abroad but has not yet been established throughout the business community. It is salutary to see at first hand the difficulties and frustrations experienced by aid and charity workers, and even by missionaries, who are sent to help in the Third World without any background in local history or knowledge of customs or social structures. The result is much waste of expensive effort.

Presentation and public speaking

Presentations are a major medium of direct communication. Unfortunately, most people are not natural public speakers and a proportion never lose a certain dread of having to face an audience, even small in-house groups.

Courses and self-training videos are helpful but it is practice, learning the importance of being briefed and prepared, that builds confidence. Command of the subject, with something to say, is the basis of a successful show. A good presentation may not win a bad argument but with the problems identified in advance, even such occasions will not lead to humiliation.

Unless one is very experienced, time spent in practice is well invested. Thirty minutes in front of a full-length mirror, making the lead points out loud, will always help. It is useful to have oneself watched, perhaps by husband or wife, or have an occasion recorded to allow identification of mannerisms that annoy or distract. Typical of such behaviour is the waving of hands, continuous scratching of the face, uncertain movement of the eyes – slight 'faults' easily to be corrected by awareness while not stilting or destroying the integrity of the performance.

Each occasion has a mood or tone. Business presentations are usually part of the operating routine but even then, an audience can be negative or bored. The mood at client and public events can be hostile. Rarely will the presenter in a commercial situation face an enthusiastic, cheering audience! On the other hand, the likely atmosphere of a business event is usually known in advance and, in anticipation of a negative situation, a speaker can come armed with a joke, a self-deprecating remark, acknowledgement of known concerns.

Training in public speaking is a sub-industry of its own, a clear indication of need. A common fault in a business situation is attempting to give the 'full story' in a limited time and then over-running. Many also speak too fast and further confuse their audience by skipping over charts and display materials too rapidly.

An audience can and will only absorb a limited amount of information from any talk or presentation – the spice should be in the words, leaving the meat to follow in written format. Unlike conversation, when people pay attention in anticipation of having to respond, the audience at a presentation can relax too much, allowing concentration to drop.

Professionals always stress that people pay attention to, and are interested in, their own concerns. The successful presenter views the subject from the perspective of the audience and is also careful to use its language. She or he is advised to identify clearly the expectations, the reasons for the occasion and only then to develop the possible solutions or the new insights for which the talk has been arranged.

There are also numerous speakers' tricks to hold attention. One is to use extreme contrast as with the cry, 'There's something criminally insane about a government that puts war before peace', or Sir Edward Heath's memorable 'the unacceptable face of capitalism'. These techniques are all taught and have their place but the best advice is to speak slowly – and, above all, to keep to time.

Most executives make only occasional presentations but these events can have an undue influence on a career. A few hours spent analysing the audience and its interests, and on reviewing personal techniques and rehearsing for the event, are a valuable personal investment.

The telephone

The telephone launched electronic communication but in spite of its ubiquity it still needs to be used with care. It is a revealing medium. People will usually make an effort during face-to-face meetings, but over the 'phone the voice reveals irritation or boredom, a lack of interest or, positively, friendliness, enthusiasm and helpfulness.

Despite its importance in communication, there is virtually no formal training for management in telephone techniques, to cultivate a professional approach and avoid the pitfalls. A customer or client is more likely to call a friendly, alert voice than one giving the impression of stress, of being imposed upon during the course of important affairs.

One simple improvement technique is to have all incoming calls recorded for a day and to let each individual have his or her own for private replay and study at home. Another is to have a researcher make dummy calls and rate a list of characteristics. These are revealing exercises.

Body language

Psychological studies suggest that individuals get 55% of information about people from body signals, 35% from voice tone and only 10% from words.

Moves such as leaning back or placing the hands pyramid fashion in front of the face are held to indicate a desire for time to think and to gain 'space'. Other movements and gestures are also open to interpretation. Eye contact can be the honest glance or, if held too long, the staring intrusion. Crossing the legs is considered to show satisfaction. The handshake can be important and worth thought and practice – not everyone is convinced by a hearty bone-crusher.

Acquaintance with these rules is certainly a help in assessing reaction and gaining understanding but there is a difficulty – people of different cultural backgrounds do not react in the same way (Chapter 9).

Also to be considered is the form of the physical contact – handshake, embrace or kiss – expected on meeting or departing. This will vary in each culture, most obviously according to the occasion, from the formal business to the light-hearted social contact, and the length of acquaintance. The experienced traveller checks what will be expected before visiting a new market.

More directly, it can be useful to review and assess behaviour generally. It can be tough but perhaps a good friend or members of the family can be asked to comment on a checklist such as that in Figure 5.2. Should a serious concern be revealed, counselling can be considered.

Appearance
- Do I look 'shower fresh'? Yes...............
  No...

Attitudes: do I come across as -
- Friendly? Yes...
  No...
- Cooperative? Yes..................................
  No...
- Open and frank? Yes...........................
  No...

Behaviour
- Do I listen? Yes...
  No...
- Express myself well? Yes.....................
  No...
- Are my manners OK? Yes.....................
  Comments..

Figure 5.2 Personality checklist.

Many of the points in the checklist can be further subdivided and there could be others about which there are personnel concerns.

WRITING AND THE COMPLETE MESSAGE

The ability to write is often considered to be deteriorating but the bulk of communication received in the office and at home is reasonably clear. Perhaps some of the criticisms come from vested interests in the educational establishment and there may be frustrated legions of potential communicators out there. Given the existing level of 'noise', however, it would seem that those able to write are producing enough as it is now.

The communicator realizes that the basis of 'good' commercial and social writing is clarity of thought and a structured approach to an objective. Clarity does not imply justification.

A common fault in business writing is the lengthy introduction setting out reasoning and explanation but confusing the message. It is usually as well to follow the style of news reports and devote the first sentence to the event, the decision and go on to detail the implications, the allocation of any responsibilities. Often the need for justification will then be seen as unnecessary but if required, perhaps for legal reasons, there can be an addendum. The main document communicates 'action' from the start.

Testing completeness

The **5W** test is a quick check for communication completeness.

- **W**hat is the subject or point?

  This implies that the subject is of interest to the addressee.
  Incidentally, scoring points, expressing anger is best confined to politics. In business, it is almost always regretted. When upset, wait a day before putting pen to fax!

- **W**here is the action taking place?
- **W**ho is involved?
- **W**hen is it all happening?
- **W**hy or how are things to be done?

In practice, the **5W** test, while also clarifying thinking, saves the embarrassment of leaving a hole in a plan, with an instruction.

It is common routine in the German-speaking world for letters to carry dual signatures, implying that the document has been read and agreed by two people. It is a valuable safeguard against the ambiguity that a sole writer close to a topic can overlook. The practice is not common in the Anglo-Saxon world but there is nothing to be lost – other than misplaced pride – and everything to gain from having a colleague check a note of importance.

The simplest sentence can have opposite meanings:

- Mr Smith, says his landlord, has given notice
- Mr Smith says his landlord has given notice

Business communication is usually intended to initiate or aid activity and does not have to stand up to scrutiny to the same extent as government material. Even so, sloppy writing is damaging and managers benefit from being reminded of the pitfalls. One way is to treat examples light-heartedly in the company magazines or have them circulated by the central desk – again with a touch of humour.

Not so funny is the failure to get across or maintain safety instructions – a finding that is not uncommon when enquiries are held into accidents. Completeness, which includes periodic review, is a very specific responsibility in this area.

Objectivity

This advertisement, expensively displayed, appeared in the UK national press.

> There is something bright on the xxx horizon. Besides the twinkling lights of its villages or in its citie's [*sic*] striking modern skyscrapers, a new bright light blazes on xxx's horizon. It's the warmth and energy blazing in the hearts of the people who are building a great nation.
>
> xxx is still the generous and community-spirited nation it always has been. And it's also a reliable partner offering outstanding possibilities for economic development and investment. We hope you'll visit and see for yourself a bright light that is bound to shine forever.
>
> xxx – A country where there is so much to see and investment opportunities awaiting.

The copy is clearly Latin in tone and presumably written by an agency in the home capital. Apart from raising a wry smile, what was it meant to achieve? Tourism and investment? Perhaps to reinforce an image of the maverick!

Much of the material for external use – the leaflets, brochures and direct mail – is produced by professionals, working with market research findings and the analysis of in-house data. The advertisement quoted above was probably the outcome of such a process but the achievement of objectivity also requires the application of common sense.

For instance, a high proportion of discretionary expenditure is now in the hands of the elderly, but all too often the type size used in material directed at this market is too small for comfortable reading by old eyes. Even with spectacles!

In mail-order advertising the juxtapositioning of illustrations, offers and coupons, in boxes with varying type faces and sizes, may delight the professional layout person – but has little chance of competing for time with the crossword on the commuter train or at the pensioner's breakfast table.

Company-wide communication, by linking everyone to the overall aims, and offering training to the individual, keeps the focus on objectivity. Written business material may not be art – although some posters, for instance, have achieved that status – but it does set out to motivate and create activity.

SELF-DEVELOPMENT AND TRAINING

The concept of self-development – for the employee to have an equal say in assessing need and choosing further training – is increasingly the norm. Training that is entirely employer-motivated may not generate the same enthusiasm and can also result in serious misunderstanding.

An individual singled out for training may quite naturally believe him- or herself to be a rising star when in fact the course has been chosen to correct a fault or overcome a problem. It is not unknown for redundancy to follow a period of further training, to the utter bewilderment of the employee.

On the other hand, given the choice, the employee may opt for personal job satisfaction or prefer to pursue an interest outside the accepted line management route. Such a move can create structural difficulties for the corporation.

In the communication environment the individual is aware of corporate objectives and, in turn, his or her personal interests are identified by the career review process. Self-development helps to align the two and build an atmosphere of trust. The result is a stronger sense of corporate identity – at a time when the life-cycle of businesses is contracting.

A feature of company decline is the inability of managements with a record of success to adapt to change. The loan records of the major US and UK financial institutions, the various boom and bust cycles in property, the high-profile niche enterprises that collapse within the decade, exemplify the break of communication with the market.

The failure of competitors can be a matter of self-congratulation among survivors but study of the underlying situation can well reveal common adverse factors. An effective self-development programme allows the rising team to help in the assessment of and preparation for change.

Top managements of leading corporations do recognize the problem of how to keep themselves in touch and apply the self-development principle by forming exclusive in-house or peer group forums for the discussion of mutual problems. Academics and recognized specialists are invited to participate or present their analyses and views of the future.

Nevertheless, horrendous mistakes are made and major corporations record losses larger than national budgets. With hindsight, the cause can appear elementary – a failure to check the quality of the earnings, the nature and make-up of stockholding or undue market exposure – effectively, a failure of communication.

Discussing the problem, one chief executive said:

> Our training programmes are for everyone, including the chief executive. You need to keep up-to-date with the changes around. If you are trying to change the culture of an organization, it is helpful to subject yourself to the training and to be seen to do so (Sir Anthony Gill, chairman of Lucas Industries).

THE COMMUNICATOR AND TRAVEL

This is a very personal view but the need for something like half of all business travel is questionable. The point is perhaps given force by the fact that travel virtually ceases, without noticeable effect on operations, during times of political tension, even when the trouble is confined to relatively remote areas.

Journeying about fills time, is felt to be 'working' when matters in the office are dragging. Contemplation, simply being quiet and thinking is not recognized as a constructive use of time. A manager can feel distinctly uneasy at being found sitting and 'doing nothing'.

Here is one comment:

> The British disease is that people are wholly task-oriented, and success is moving one pile of paper from an 'in' tray to an 'out' tray.
>
> Some people feel uncomfortable just sitting at a desk thinking. They should be doing it for a more significant part of their day. Otherwise, how do you say to yourself that you're giving the right direction and the emphasis to the things you're doing? (Peter Middleton, chief executive of Lloyd's).

Pointers to unnecessary travel include a sparse agenda, or none at all, and frequent changes of schedules and itinerary.

Company-wide communication, on the other hand, alleviates this tyranny of action. The flow of data and contact with colleagues is well established.

Of course, visits are an integral communication element and sometimes – but not as often as claimed – five minutes' conversation (except it is never that brief) can replace a month's correspondence. For trips to be successful, the agenda needs to be agreed and the plans firm, allowing appointments to be made, data to be collected, and materials prepared. A first-time visitor will also study the market environment data held on the central databanks.

Overall, the policy manual sets out the travel procedure, from approval, through preparation to reporting back and updating the databases.

The subject is perhaps brought into perspective by a story Martin French of Credit Lyonnais Securities likes to tell. A trio of Chinese diviners, hired as a publicity gag, went on to predict the movements of the Hong Kong stock market with near-perfect accuracy. 'It makes you wonder why we employ large teams of analysts', he comments.

The same can, one feels, be said on occasion of business travel.

SUMMARY

'Positive' listening is a good base from which to build communication skills.

Current organizational trends require a move from passive to active communication. Individuals must take much of the initiative but encouragement for improvement comes with a system of career reviews.

Characteristics important to communicating and building empathy include personal appearance and an understanding of the use of language, in conversation, for public speaking, on the telephone. Written communication is tested for completeness and objectivity.

The communicator uses self-development and training programmes to enhance these skills and to build the self-confidence that frees him or her from the 'tyranny of action'.

6

COMMUNICATION AND OFFICE POLITICS

Vain hope to make men happy by politics (Carlyle).

Effective company-wide communication seeks to harness office politics – whether the opportunism of the Sparrow or the careful planning of the Falcon – to the achievement of the corporate programme. The chief executive has a strong interest in a network that will identify talent and ability.

INTRODUCTION

The times are egalitarian, legal protection has strengthened, the basis of employment improved, but for the majority, work is still just that, a routine for earning a living.

A growing proportion, however, have a wider horizon of opportunity. Operating units are becoming smaller, more positions are skilled and the trend is clear – increasingly people are seeking and jobs are offering career prospects. Fiction and the journalist love the steamy business romance and delight in exposing an office ogre. Undoubtedly such aspects of life do affect positioning but it is hard ambition that is the spur for real-politik in the workplace.

KEEPING POLITICS POSITIVE

Politics is by no means equated with negative activity: by sharpening internal competition, bringing talent to the fore, political activity plays a role in building the enterprise. Although often held out as the machinations of individuals selfishly seeking personal advantage, politics also encompass the skill that builds cooperation and gets things done. The slimmed-down organizations of the technological age do not offer much opportunity for wicked scheming. The ability to influence and thus to shape events is more likely to be a corporate asset than a divisive negative.

Effective communication is the tool with which the individual harnesses politics to endeavour and ability. In the team environment, political skills facilitate the joint effort; in the hierarchical organization, political activity becomes more personal. Without being seen as 'astutely contriving and intriguing', the ambitious will work on links with:

- the line manager;
- top management;
- the (presumed) rising star;
- colleagues, as allies and rivals.

Individual relationships take time to develop, reactions are not predictable and chance digs numerous pitfalls. Character and ambition have been classified in many modes but, in the search for the best path, the office politician tends to operate in one of two modes. The Sparrow is continually anxious, attuned to analysing every nuance. He is watchful to avoid association with mistakes or disaster, perhaps more so than seeking to link with success.

The Falcon, on the other hand, is more of a strategist, calmly working a campaign plan towards identified goals. Other 'species', particularly the malicious and disruptive, are in a separate category, with their activity hopefully kept at a low ebb by the open communication of a company-wide network.

The reverse side, the corporate interest, is clear: to harness political activity towards the productive and to minimize if not avoid the damaging divisiveness of personality conflicts, both overt and covert. Politics, the 'acting or proceeding in accordance with good policy', is integral to organization. One definition of management is that it is the art of achieving objectives through other people, and that is inherently a political activity.

In the company-wide communication environment, with the free flow of data and the consultation procedures, the scope for disruptive politics is reduced. At the same time, the political moves of management in the making of choice and the allocation of priorities are better understood through the open budget procedures and the regular updating of the workforce.

COMMUNICATION WITH THE LINE MANAGER

The relationship between a manager and his or her people is to a large degree dependent on communication. Inevitably there will be perceived or actual favouritism, the essence of disruptive personal politics, and resentment of the colleague thought to be currying favour with the boss.

An insecure manager may feel bolstered by the sycophant or, frustrated by any one of a score of factors – vested interests, indecisions elsewhere or clashing personalities – can be happy to lean on or use the willing shoulder. Alternatively, he or she can 'rule by fear', bullying subordinates with any number of techniques, from creating insecurity by continually changing instructions to actually lying about what is being done or has happened.

The Sparrow sees the opportunity for a hop, perhaps only to offer sympathy but, more postively, to come up with ideas and suggestions. For the Falcon, a weak manager, or one beset by difficulties, is prey – opening access to higher management. A word here, a hint there and a barrier to progress in the shape of the weakling might be removed.

The activities of the Sparrow and the Falcon may well be helpful overall in solving a given situation, perhaps in exposing the bully – but their activities should not be necessary. Given a workplace where everyone is linked into the internal communication network, most positively in this respect through a consultation procedure, each is kept in touch with progress and has the opportunity to participate in the further development of the programme. In turn, the system keeps management in tune with the operational atmosphere, the morale of the organization. No manager operates, or is allowed to work, in isolation: through the network each one is part of the team.

THE CHIEF EXECUTIVE AND COMMUNICATION

It can be lonely at the top, the target of everyone with ambition. In all likelihood, the chief executive, probably a leading Falcon in his or her time, now finds the chair surrounded by a hungry flock. Perhaps there are also other Falcons to be seen watching from outside. Assessment of the quality of his or her communications now becomes the daily concern: just how correct and complete is the information arriving on the desk? What else is happening that has not been said or is not known? The 'areas of the unknown' are always out there, threatening: how efficient are the external communication links?

Internally, given personal experience of political in-fighting, an important question has to be: is success being acknowledged correctly and being encouraged further? Identification of the contributors and the innovators is a key concern for the chief but the claiming of credit can be ruthless. In the process valuable people can be lost. The reverse is equally a concern: are mistakes and problems being fully reported and their source properly identified?

Both the Sparrow and the Falcon are ever watchful of success, guarding their own and seeking to be at least associated, if more is not possible, with that of others. The Falcon may well have identified potential areas of success – a new product line, an exciting innovation, the capture of an important account – and taken care to be linked with the development, to be seen to participate and hopefully be recognized as the prime mover. The Sparrow has a sharp eye for the immediate opportunity and will seek to seize it. Every executive has seen the analysis, the detailed recommendations for further development, compiled after initial experience has assured the success of a project.

Identifying talent

A chief executive needs the assurance of an efficient internal network for identifying talent and achievement. A primary concern of the continuous process of renewal and change has to be exploitation of the best and brightest minds and a chief executive must be sure of what is available to the organization.

He or she should also have a second major objective, that of identifying the successor. There are strong arguments, not least those relating to personal health and the ability to remain innovative, for limited tenure of the chief executive office. A good person will start finding and grooming a successor from the time of his or her own appointment and will make that clear to the internal team.

While in office, the ability to manage corporate politics positively is an important requirement of a chief executive. Division and broken relationships are signs of failure, most often in terms of communication. Mark Fuller, president of the Monitor Company, a consultancy based in Cambridge, Massachusetts, says:

> In most cases I see, not only are the majority of the problems political, but the proportion is growing. Companies have greater technical resources ... **but that kind of expertise cannot help if there are taboos on sharing or even collecting certain information, or when the truth dare not be told**.

The Monitor Company grew into a world consultancy in the decade after it was established in 1983. The founders were individuals overtly seeking escape from other politicized organizations. In a press account, Fuller has described how the founding group almost came to grief early on as the original partners, who had been determined to be open and straightforward, in fact reinvented politics in their manoeuvring against each other.

It took a Harvard professor, Chris Argyris, to help re-establish the structure, a key element of the rescue being the introduction of a system of consultation. The managing group was made to meet regularly, not only to discuss the business but also to assess the contributions of each individual, including the performance of the chief executive himself. Resentments and frustrations are not allowed to fester.

Fuller has found that the root of much trouble lies in defensive stratagems, people avoiding problems or hiding mistakes and seeking to distance themselves from failures. Insistence on openness and exposure both to what is happening and of feelings, even in regard to the activities of the chief executive, avoids turning a difficulty into a threat. Defusing emotion and overcoming problems by positive action comes with the confidence that over time is engendered by open, consultative communication.

Difficulties that seem overwhelming to the executive involved are put into perspective by the group; team experience teaches the mature approach and provides the encouragement of support from his or her peers for the individual.

The changing game plan

The chief executive faces a continually changing game plan. He or she might, for example, be recommended to create a new department or entity. Is the suggestion meeting a real need or opportunity? Perhaps a Falcon sees this as an extension of his or her power base or as enhancing the prospects for promotion. Alternatively, the new venture could sidetrack a rival.

Despite the power play, is the proposal one of value? The shifting alignment of resources, finance, production and manpower, is a reflection of the struggles to be expected between leading personalities operating normally in the real world. The chief executive him- or herself is threatened should the pressures come from outside, as when a predator, identifying weaknesses left unattended or not noticed by the established team, sees the possibility for profit.

Conglomerates, such as Hanson, are built in this way and not even the largest corporation is safe. Mere speculation in the press that Hanson had recognized opportunities and possible alternatives at ICI led the industrial giant into a fundamental re-organization. The company was split into two, management doing just what it assumed the predator's plan to be. Meanwhile, Hanson sold its stake at a satisfactory profit.

Such events highlight the political weakness of the traditional structure, one in which communication is largely confined to formal reporting through line management. The system is designed to run operations and monitor results but does not mobilize company-wide thinking, nor does it probe continually into the 'areas of the unknown', the guard against complacency. No matter how unique or powerful the business, change is continuing and will overwhelm the unwary.

Despite a historic 80% of the world market, IBM faced an immense problem in moving from giant mainframe computers into the environment of the personal machine. It is ironic, but serves to make the point, that the world provider of communication technology has itself been found wanting in regard to internal communication. The warnings of the growing momentum of change were simply not absorbed by the corporation.

In bad times, an effective network warns the chief executive of internal criticism and external hostility, whether against him- or herself or in the form of a threat to the corporation as well. In facing difficulties, it is natural for immediate problems to become dominant but company-wide communication brings help from two sources. First, the entire workforce is involved and expected to contribute towards solutions. In parallel, monitoring of the environment, of the 'areas of the unknown', is designed to capture whatever might be helpful from the outside.

No one has a greater interest in the building and maintenance of the communication network than the chief executive. He or she has only themself to blame when caught unawares. In building the network and by fostering the internal structure, it is the chief executive whose attitude directly determines the quality of the intelligence he or she receives.

THE HIGH-FLIER

Alert and professional management is continuely in search of the outstanding individual, who might or might not be politically aware and could well be enmeshed in a web of rival interests. The corporate aim is first to identify ability and achievement, and then to ensure its development and retention. The politically aware individual seeks recognition and can guard against being overshadowed by an ambitious Falcon or being shared out among the Sparrows.

On the other hand, the politicians, whether Sparrow or Falcon, are also alert to the rising star and, if circumstances allow, aim at alliance. There will be support of proposals at meetings and the sharing of information, generally maintaining a high profile with the target individual. Alternatively, those who feel threatened, whether as jealous rivals or as managers ahead of the upstart, can seek to block the 'star's' progress. Proposals will be ignored or re-presented in another format, access to key events hindered and achievements obscured.

Situations are seldom clear-cut and some of the reasoning behind such manoeuvring may be well-founded and even beneficial to the enterprise. However, objectivity can be lost when discussion is limited, whether in scope or participation; forward thinking and the successful handling of change demands the open consultation inherent in the company-wide communication environment.

Great technical expertise stands out and is recognized but a high-flier has often to build and keep a profile, to develop a Falcon plan. The communication network provides the tools. The internal channels are used to keep abreast of the budget situation, the progress with individual schemes and projects, and to assess the opportunities for contributing further. Meanwhile, care can be taken to ensure that reports, results and projects are fully recorded throughout the system, known up and down the line and in the organization generally.

The external network is also monitored continually in order to stay in touch, both to learn of what is happening and to probe as far as possible into what is foreseen. A high-flyer often emerges by identifying the new, achieving an alliance or introducing a major innovation.

It is also valuable to establish a reputation in the industry, with the trade, or among suppliers, to become a recognized figure for getting things done, for willingness to help, or for ideas and innovation.

A further task is to keep abreast of the non-commercial network. The high-flier understands that political and environmental developments can be vital and makes every effort to establish personal links with important or potentially influential people outside the business. The ability to bring in the broader view at a budget session, during a tight commercial discussion, to be able to point to the possible reaction of an environmental group or of the trade, will make a mark.

Great design or chance?

The business textbooks ignore the element of chance: it is a factor too destructive of reasoned argument and analysis, the antithesis of the clear solution. While the world of business has remain oblivious and training entirely disregards it, the theory of Chaos has given birth to a whole new discipline. The famous Lorenz butterfly that changes the weather of the globe with the beat of a wing has yet to make an impact on business thinking.

A high-flier, more so the Falcon planner, will not ignore the randomness of chaos in the lives of people and their organizations. He or she will be prepared to pause, not fear to be seen to be devoting time to study and thinking, perhaps to projecting the impossible. More directly, the imaginative will speculate on the 'areas of the unknown': what can be foreseen, within reason and unreasonably? This naturally leads on to contingency planning, however tentative, to deal with and mitigate the effects of the impossible, when it happens.

Although the warning signs had become ever more ominous over a period of at least 20 years none, at least no one at the head of foreign offices or in the boardrooms of the oil giants, foresaw the 1973 oil crisis. Presumably position papers and assessments had moved up and around the channels of communication but these were ignored or their contents found so outlandish as to be unabsorbable.

The result was the misery of thousands of bankruptcies and a crisis that threatened the entire financial structure of the world. The Sparrows, of course, saw the opportunity, came out in force and made fortunes in spot trading, the supply of niche markets.

A handful of major corporations, such as du Pont, retain a noted personality to think the impossible. Others are members of high-level think tanks but there the agendas tend to the more predictable medium- and longer-term scenarios. The potential of thinking the impossible remains largely unexplored. 'It will never happen here' is certainly wrong but such projection ahead is discouraged because history shows that prediction is also usually mistaken. That is not the point, of course; opportunity lies in being aware that there will be change and in maintaining the flexibility to handle it.

COMMUNICATION WITH COLLEAGUES AND RIVALS

Standing out in the crowd, making a mark, is the first priority of ambitious politicians. The continuing machinations of the malicious or the activity of the troublemaker is not for them: it is ideas and success, their own and such as they can capture, for which recognition is sought.

Sparrows, ever alert and hopping from viewpoint to viewpoint, scan the ground for crumbs. They are likely to be conscious of the trappings of office, and to them status and function are communicated by the size of the room, the fixtures and facilities and, above all, in the use of the car.

It is extraordinary but for many at every level, from the boardroom to the salesperson, the car is still see as communicating personal status and evidence of having 'arrived'. As any personnel manager will testify, more blood, and not only that of Sparrows, is spilt over the car than on any other condition of employment.

For the Sparrow, any change or nuance of alteration in the conditions of service is analysed and examined politically: what is 'their' objective, and are there advantages to be further exploited or disadvantages to be guarded against, now immediately or in the more distant future?

Here is one source of rumour and gossip. Unless all change is fully explained, there will be speculation and worse as the malicious, seeking someone's discomfort, undermine morale and divert effort. Ineffective communication, any gap in the network, is quickly filled by the rumour grapevine – almost entirely negative to the corporate interest of concentrating attention on the tasks in hand.

Organizations that have poor or no consultative process may well use the grapevine to float proposals in order to check reactions and measure likely support or opposition. It is but a poor substitute for an effective internal network, a negation of professional management. Communication through a grapevine – it has been described as 'the black market for information' – is out of the control of management and tends to emphasize the destructive.

Rumour will have the board at loggerheads, the new product a failure and reorganization and personality changes imminent. It is not the background from which successful teams emerge.

SUMMARY

Politics is a normal feature of the workplace and, the malicious apart, not necessarily destructive.

Line managers and senior executives, themselves players, are the targets of the ambitious and the high-flier. Meanwhile, the prime interest of the chief executive is accurate and complete intelligence.

The organizational structure does not need and seeks to minimize politicking and its associated grapevine of rumour. Alert and professional management operates through a network of open consultation and communication.

7

THE INTERNAL COMMUNICATION NETWORK

All media are used to build the internal communication network. Staff involvement and input, management and use of the intelligence is kept under continued surveillance by a director or senior executive.

INTRODUCTION

The director responsible for communication ensures the full availability of each link of the network (Table 7.1), establishes the programme of data input and management and periodically checks the entire function with the Communication Health Index. Every employee is a communicator.

THE PHYSICAL LINKS OF THE NETWORK

The internal company-wide network uses every medium as a two-way channel of communication.

Table 7.1 Links of the communication network

Link   Potential for communication
                              (rating: xxx - 0)

	Penetration	Timely	Easy use	'Human'
Terminals	xxx	xxx	xx	x - 0
Consult group	xxx	xx	xx	xxx
Publications	xxx	x	xxx	x
Reports and returns	x	xx	xx	x
Meetings and conferences	xx	xx	x	xx
Informal contact	x	x	0	xxx

The terminals

In addition to their use in direct operations, the terminals give access to both in-house and external data, carry the electronic mail and other information, including 'noticeboard' announcements and company news and updates. The terminals also allow direct contact with management and access to in-house specialist expertise or indicate where further help is available.

In turn, the terminals are used to update customer/client files and the relevant records of stocks or work in progress. A complete system also holds a database for comments, complaints, customer reactions and for recording intelligence on market developments.

Consultative groups

Company-wide communication has every employee a member of a group in the consultative system. The prime function is discussion and review by operating personnel both of the job and of the working environment. In turn, the groups are used as sounding boards for plans, proposals and possible developments. Active and full use of consultative groups helps to give the workplace its human face.

The process is not a counter to established trade unionism but a separate, purely in-house system of communication. The ideal is close liaison between the two.

Publications

Every company or organization of any size maintains contact with each employee by way of magazines or newsletters. Ideally, a given publication will review the overall corporate situation, discuss plans and developments (not ignoring problems) and also focus on the interests of the immediate office or operation. Publications that are used only as a medium for enhancing the corporate self-image and detailing success (perhaps adding human interest with a little social news) are failing to exploit the opportunities offered by print.

To hold attention and be recognized as an honest vehicle, internal publications must be at least as informative as the reports of analysts or the news published in the press. In turn, the columns are open to employee input, both to raise 'Agony Aunt' queries on benefits and working conditions, and also to give space to the broader corporate issues – the 'why don't we, why are we not doing ...?' discussion.

Reports and returns

There is an established routine for reports and returns, which will also be set out in the policy manual. Within an office, the use of data can be enhanced by having records accessible or by circulating a day-file of current correspondence.

The communication cycle is completed by regular acknowledgement, reply and feedback from management, possibly arranged by the central desk. Relevant operational data noted in the reports, on clients, the markets and technology, is entered into the databases by the central desk for access through the departmental terminals.

Meetings and conferences

The annual round of internal meetings is established by the planning and budget cycle. Much of this activity is of direct operational interest only but the outcome, in the form of plans and the agreed objectives of the budget, is entered into the network. The conclusions of special events and conferences on particular issues are often of interest to a wider circle than the participating group and summarized minutes, or listings of what is available in the relevant offices, are also noted on the operational database.

Informal contact

A managed company-wide network recognizes the value of informal contact, both in the day-to-day routine but also as a medium of consultation and data exchange. People are encouraged to meet, particularly by the provision of appropriate meal and canteen facilities. A couple of chairs at a coffee machine might not seem much but such little attentions help create the communication atmosphere; people realize they are expect to talk, to make contact and help each other. It is a common experience to find that a casual encounter has produced the seed of a useful idea.

DATA INPUT TO THE NETWORK

Data input to the company-wide network is continuous but a practical start point can be the period when planning is briefly halted and the operating budget has finally been approved (after the usual anguish) by management. Each unit now has its documented operational plan: the sales director will align the sales force, set product targets by outlet and territory; the marketing team starts implementing the promotional programme by tactic, time period and medium; and the whole complexity of activity moves forward into the new business period.

From this point on, performance is communicated in the form of financial statements and general progress monitored by the market reports.

Communicating the objectives

In an environment of company-wide communication awareness of the plans and objectives is not confined to the relevant operating management. In broad terms at least, the targets for the coming year are held on the internal information **database**. The chief executive will also set out the plans and his or her objectives in the **magazines**. Subsequently, space will be devoted to special situations, new projects and progress to date as the year unfolds.

It is more stimulating and creative of a sense of common purpose to **present** the plans directly to each group and operation. It is still common for a workforce, carrying on the routine from day-to-day, to be unaware of, and consequently unconcerned with the current objectives, never mind the overall strategy. Even the lower levels of management may have only a limited view of the corporate purpose – and, **in effect, the great majority is cut off from contributing more than immediate and disinterested labour.**

The human resource, the one resource of infinite capacity and capability, is not being exploited to the full.

The planning process does not go far down the operational line, and effectively ignores much of the talent available to the enterprise. There is no reason why foremen and section heads should not be required to budget their operation. Relatively little extra effort is involved in breaking out the forms and paperwork one or two stages further but, if the process is considered too cumbersome, then at least these experienced people can be brought into the discussions, asked to consider costs and suggest improvements.

Planning, budgeting and re-forecasting consumes more of management time than does any other activity and to widen the process by involving yet more people and other levels, might seem to be devoting even greater resources to the process. There are, however, two distinct advantages:

1. A budget built up from the estimates of the smallest operational cell can be considered relatively firm and realistic. This should save time later in the year by reducing the need for continuing revision of the figures – often the most frustrating of management tasks.
2. Broadening the input to the budgeting process taps all the available talent. Sharp ideas and proposals can come from the youngest or the most junior. In the process, the team is built, everyone is committed to the objectives.

Company-wide communication also provides for the operating plans, once finalized, to be presented to each unit, preferably at the start of each cycle and by a senior executive. It is an important occasion and one that clearly demonstrates the commitment to the team approach.

It is not a one-off show. Given the effort put into regular review of budget status – achievement to date against plan – throughout the year the commitment to communication simply requires that a little of the time is devoted to keeping up the interest, hopefully the enthusiasm of the workforce. Senior executives talk to their people – and are seen to be treating them as people, as partners in the enterprise.

It pays off in every way, in enthusiasm, cooperation and with commitment. Many a manager, having had the expense and loss of modifying a plan, changing a procedure in the light of experience, then finds that the solution has been there all the time, in the workforce. The problem simply had not been posed to those directly involved – worse, the mechanism for doing so did not exist.

The team approach – empowerment

The heralded alternative to the traditional hierarchical organization is for operations to be run by self-managing teams. These need have no leader and the supervising executive or director is scheduled to act more in the role of a consultant than a manager. Direct intervention comes only when the budget goes awry. The system is built on open communication. As the teams can operate only if fully informed and kept in touch with the experience of other groups, the flow of intelligence has to be continuous.

With responsibility being both joint and individual, the members of a team have also to be in close touch with one another. The difficulties with a product or a client cannot be ignored or left for someone else to discover, but must be brought out and resolved. Day-to-day work patterns have to be agreed by the team members.

The teams have to be given their targets and briefed on market conditions and the customer structure, and fully trained as regards the products or services. There is contact with corporate back-up, the media advertising, research and product development and suppliers. In turn, a system of reporting and monitoring results is established and there is a requirement for feedback on the market, customer reactions and product performance. It is an environment of continuous communication (see Figure 5.1).

Operating the budget

The media used to communicate the budget – direct presentation, the magazines, the information database – continue to be the vehicles for reporting progress throughout the year.

Obviously, communication of accurate and timely financial information is the first essential to running a budget. Where the planning process has started 'down the line', every operating unit and product group, the individual specialists and the technical functions are aware of the hurdles to be overcome for objectives to be met; for them to continue contributing fully, each has to be kept informed of what is happening, of the progress to date.

The finance department is geared to serving management and

meeting statutory requirements but it does not exist for these purposes alone. It has also to report to and guide every operational unit. There are practical limits to the distribution of financial data but communication needs to be sufficient for the smallest unit to have a full understanding of what it is achieving and of its contribution to overall objectives.

One result of the publication of achievement by unit is to foster healthy internal 'competition', each operation vying to achieve the best results. Everyone and not only the manager is given an element of personal interest, adding a welcome dynamic into the routine of the workplace.

The stimulation of budget accountability is proved when the concept is introduced to social organizations, medical facilities, schools and universities. An early change was in the USA, where under the MAC (Maximum Allowable Cost) system, providers of health care are reimbursed according to a fixed-charge formula for a given condition and its treatment. It is an area of some complexity but the formula quickly succeeded in communicating the implications of health care – to the patient, the suppliers and the professions.

Even in the extreme case of the British National Health Service, where in principle all is 'free' at the point of consumption, hospital administrators, doctors and specialist functions are increasingly expected to work within budgets and to compete for revenue by offering services at lower costs.

The centrally controlled economies of the former Soviet Russian empire were run without budget or communicative planning. The arbitrary setting of production targets, divorced both from resources and the market, resulted in waste and loss on such a stupendous scale that shortage and non-availability were the norm. It is ironic that the ability of individuals to accept responsibility and meet challenge was not recognized or accepted by a system ostensibly based on an ideology created for that very purpose.

Consultative groups

The structure of consultation varies widely. The broadest is the Japanese concept of *kaizen* or continuous improvement, which has the workers in each section holding a meeting every morning. The routine of the previous day is considered, with everyone given the chance to participate, and the results are then passed on to the immediate management. Discussion is not limited to the processes of work but also takes account of the human factor, of the difficulties and frustrations of the individual.

Another structure has every worker taking part in courses designed over perhaps three days, both to explain and clarify the corporate objectives and to introduce the consultation procedure. Employees are then encouraged to form voluntary groups that meet regularly to discuss operations and perhaps invite a management presence. Experience has shown that, when well founded, the groups often develop a social dimension, e.g. offer support to members in times of personal difficulty. A wider participation in communal affairs can also grow – perhaps in the arrangement of blood donations or help with a local need.

People get directly involved and the results can be measured: alcoholism and absenteeism fall and punctuality improves; work patterns are voluntarily synchronized to meet situations that would otherwise disrupt output; individuals are conscious of their responsibilities to their fellows and the group.

There is much scope for innovation. One novel approach is to create shadow executive groups or boards of directors from junior and middle managers. These groups operate with the real-life agenda: monitoring current progress to correct areas of weakness or further exploit success, plan ahead and fix investment priorities, arrange finance and plan for people.

A group meets regularly, perhaps monthly, and has the results minuted and reviewed by the actual executive committee. A senior manager 'minds' the group, acts as liaison between the two, and while remaining an observer, helps to keep the discussion focused, steered away from the procedural or academic.

Experience of the real-life problems faced by the corporation opens up new perspectives for the juniors, and builds their management and analytical skills. Members note the actual gain of inter-departmental communication in working with colleagues.

As one participant put it: 'I now know much more about what is happening in other departments and since we look at issues through departmental eyes – the finance angle, the marketing angle and so on – you get to understand what drives them, what they are trying to achieve and the problems they face.'

The actual executive team benefits from the insight into the views and thinking of the rising generation – even if it is not quite as valuable as the claim that 'We can make top management consider things they would not otherwise have looked at. We see a lot that senior management doesn't.'

Table 7.2 shows the direct returns that involving the workforce in consultation brings.

Table 7.2 Involving the workforce

Input	Return
Objectives and change	Ideas
Budget	Productivity
Progress	Commitment

Trade unions

Trade union contact is determined to an important extent by external factors but in part could be considered to run in parallel with the consultation process. Companies that recognize trade unions have historic communication procedures in place and the company-wide network does not seek to undermine them.

While trends towards smaller operating units, more skilled, flexible and individualized working patterns tend to erode traditional unionism, the basic objectives of secure and improving employment remain common ground. The achievement of a good working relationship between the unions and the internal network has to be a particular element of the communication portfolio. The situation can be individual or industry-wide but it is one in which the communication of change, through regular contact, can be of particular significance. A good start is to have the internal workforce fully aware of what is happening to the organization and in the marketplace.

Staff contacts

The employees are an under-used resource in one respect – in the exploitation of private interests and positions. Legal restraints apart, a voluntary listing of staff interests on a database can open up corporate opportunities: a valuable contact, a much-sought opening may be possible through a colleague on the next floor. Personal interests in sport, music and other hobbies attract people from all walks of life and employees may well have contacts of value, far above their own level of employment.

Typical comment on the staff resource came in a review of safety at London Transport when it was realized that it was not known how much of the collective experience was being tapped, nor if the best knowledge available had been incorporated in the crisis manuals. 'Someone may have a skill, but it may not be known that he has the skill,' noted one executive.

The suggestion box

An established communication technique is that of the suggestion box, through which one and all are encouraged to put forward ideas, particularly for improvements in procedures and processes. Useful suggestions are rewarded and publicized, possibly by public presentations, more often in the magazines.

The procedure can, with discretion, be applied more widely. Given the protection of some form of coding or the use of a neutral channel, such as the financial auditors, the 'box' can be a route for questioning organizational procedures. Clearly this is a delicate area but results can be useful. Loopholes 'on the ground' in the control of e.g. transport, stocks or purchases, that may not be obvious to management, perhaps in a period of reorganization or change, are brought to light before serious loss.

COMMUNICATION AND MANAGEMENT PRODUCTIVITY

Intuition and flair are key elements of success – but, unfortunately, are not available to order and, in any event, have some foundation of knowledge and understanding. An obvious truism is that the great generality of activity is based on information and the better the data the more likely the happy outcome.

Much of management communication is face-to-face, both at formal meetings and, equally important, during the course of informal contact. The formal includes the regular departmental and budget progress meetings and the 'by need' events arranged at each stage of a project. These intertwine with the annual cycle of planning and budgeting.

The formal meeting

In the communication environment, meetings are 'open' so that, apart from those directly involved, others who might benefit or contribute are free to join, their schedules permitting. The accountant attending a sales conference, a production director sitting in on a marketing campaign presentation, or product chiefs at regional and factory meetings, all widen their horizons. The 'outsiders' may well be able to contribute and ask a relevant question and, in turn, see opportunities for adjusting their own operations and procedures to fit better into the overall operation.

It is also communication network routine for the conclusions of or notes on the important gatherings to be generally available to the appropriate circle, either by direct distribution or on request. However, managers are busy, possess varying communication skills and differing perspectives and cannot be expected to think through and undertake such a task for all their documentation. Instead, the central desk is copied and has the responsibility of either extracting and circulating the relevant information or 'advertising' what is available – fulfilling the important role of networking.

Within a department or office the objective can be achieved by having the messages and letters copied to a day file, which is either circulated to every desk or – and this is administratively easier – made accessible to all executives.

Informal contact and networking

Informal contact is continuous – the discussion in the corridor, the chat on the telephone or in a colleague's office are all inherent features of the daily routine. At the same time, the structure can foster or hinder casual contact, easing or discouraging a desirable level of relationships.

The whole purpose of getting people together in an office is for them to communicate and work together. The prime aim of all office layout is not to achieve a nice decor, the latest facilities, important as these are, but to have the staff harmoniously in touch with each other, to facilitate contact at every interface.

In practice, each operating unit has an atmosphere, developed over time and with little conscious provision for comfortable personal communication. The office was set up with some thought as to functional convenience but has since remained essentially unaltered or adjusted piecemeal to accommodate new personnel and equipment.

In the communication environment, office layout is also subject to periodic review, perhaps best done along with all the other operational features, at budget time. There is a hidden but real cost in poorly arranged offices, in terms of wasted time, frustration, under-used facilities and equipment. Making do to accommodate an extra person or meet a change is not sufficient.

A feature that is not always considered is provision of the 'social area' – the unobtrusive space at the coffee machine or a chair or two in a convenient corner, perhaps near the lifts. Here people run into each other, pause to exchange thoughts and pass on ideas. Gossiping can appear wasteful and indulgent – but it is one way in which people grow together, develop mutual understanding and go on to build a team.

It is also how many ideas are born.

Meals and breaks

The staff facilities are obvious points of informal contact. An attractive canteen can encourage executives to leave their desks and meet for a break; alternatively, where tea and coffee are served individually, these periods can be recognized for informal 'visiting'.

There is no justification for segregated meal facilities between different levels of employee. It may well be necessary to have entertainment rooms and a canteen separate from and at a lower price than the dining room, but each is open to everyone. Useful links are established, often across rigid departmental lines, when it is not unusual for senior managers to take canteen lunches.

Equally, employees, key workers and section heads in particular, are encouraged to use, and made to feel at home in the restaurant – and to talk when they are there. People get to know each other across the organizational spectrum and become used to talking.

The communicating of mistakes

A most difficult area is the communication of mistakes, first in having them admitted, whether by the corporation or an individual, and then in learning from them. There is no welcome for the bearer of bad news and the instinct is to hide or deny a mistake – leaving the damage to fester or to have it repeated. The fault may lie in an outdated system but nobody is given the opportunity to hear of it and change matters.

The inventor of instant photography and founder of Polaroid, Ed Land, had this sign on his wall: 'A mistake is an event the full benefit of which has not yet been turned to your advantage.'

It is the culture of the pioneer, who recognizes that mistakes are inevitable but insists on their being part of the educational process. Every element in the company-wide communication environment strives to build openness and the trust that will allow mistakes to surface. There is no fear of retribution, deserved or otherwise – unless a mistake has been hidden.

Health

The health of senior managers, of the chief executive is another area of great difficulty, where the individual's right to privacy can conflict with the corporate good. In the US, public companies have to report facts 'material' to the business – and at least two chief executives of major corporations have in the recent past immediately and openly announced catastrophic diagnoses. Others have not and have died in harness but some time after having ceased to be effective.

The peer consultative group should be confident enough to handle questions of health but there is a natural reluctance to pry into such a deeply personal area. The ideal is to have it as a matter of contract that each top executive must submit an annual health report – just as is required of airline pilots.

MANAGING THE DATA

The central desk

Much of the 'raw' data required by the corporation are captured by, or can be arranged to become part of, the daily routine of field reports and internal assessments. Intelligence is also gathered from trade and industry sources and events, publications and press. Although overseen by a director, the management of communication also requires a central desk, necessarily situated in the executive office, from where the system is monitored on a daily basis and the flow and relevance of the data assessed.

The central desk also plays a key role in the distribution of information. Here the responsible executive is aware of company-wide activity and can judge whether material has and is being correctly and fully circulated. Additionally, extracted data is published in a newsletter or put out over the terminals and notice is given of available documentation, e.g. minutes of meetings and notes on events and conferences.

Personalities are always involved but a central desk, run sympatheti-cally by an experienced manager, becomes an apolitical point of contact, a communication link in its own right.

The databanks

The internal data apart, the terminal also links each desk to the ever-growing banks of specialist and external information. The individual manager has difficulty in staying abreast of all that is happening, and becoming available, and not everything that looks 'interesting' is in fact useful. Data services can be expensive, particularly so if the intelli-gence is not used. The explosion in available data and intelligence (Figure 7.1) carries with it the danger of overwhelming the individual. Continued analyses, reformulations and projections can lead to the relevant facts being lost. The communication audit should both ques-tion the usefulness of data (whether generated internally or purchased from outside) and check that it is being used effectively.

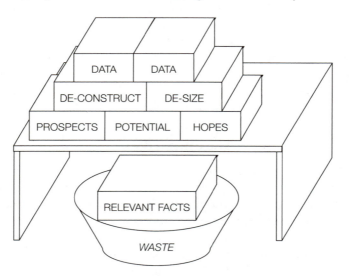

Figure 7.1 The data explosion.

One role of the central desk is to understand and be aware of infor-mation needs across the organization, not a difficult task given access to plans and budgets and the routine copying of reports and data. It then becomes possible to advise on new material that comes on offer. For example, a trade-mark file, available to the head office legal department, may well be helpful to a country manager checking names and marks for his or her product development programme.

On the other hand there is the pressure to buy new sources of data, not only from the suppliers but also originating internally, from staff naturally keen to access the latest information available.

There is not a corporation without its data horror stories, usually reflecting diffused management responsibility. Even where expenditure is within individual departmental budget limits waste is avoided by a central check, both as to cost-benefit and to avoid overlapping purchase. Meanwhile, the environment is constantly changing and with it the scope and depth of the intelligence required – today's monitors may quickly become obsolete.

The review of databank access, the depth and relevance of what is to hand and what else has become available, is part of the routine of planning but also a continuing responsibility of the central desk and of the director holding the communication portfolio.

Security

Security is also an element of their remit. Systems become more complex – and more accessible. Internal mistakes take their toll but deliberate malfeasance and outright sabotage are (stated to be) the cause of enormous loss. The estimates usually originate with suppliers of security systems but real losses are also documented, such as those suffered by a Californian insurance company that left a dismissed operator in the computer room and found every file wiped clean.

Developing the personnel function

Terms of employment will always be on the management agenda. It is ironic that while area and product managers and all operations are expected to update and develop the new, the personnel office, dealing with the key 'raw material', can be left alone, to plod on from year to year outside the discipline of the planning cycle.

The internal communication of employee benefits, pension and health provisions and training programmes deserves attention equivalent to that given to a product and service marketing plan.

For an international corporation, some of the issues, such as pensions and health provision, cannot be equated across markets. In the communication environment, there are parameters and guidelines to reassure the dispersed operations that equitable treatment is sought across the world. Such forethought and provision become important when it proves necessary to answer political charges at home or, in a foreign legislature, to meet criticism from a pressure group.

The directors

The directors and top executives are an under-used communication resource. In parallel to their executive role, directors are ambassadors to the employees and to the outside world. Running the business includes recognizing the responsibility to communicate, a task not entirely delegated to the personnel department and professional public relations people.

Business chiefs could do worse than study the ability and willingness of politicians to speak out at the front. Traditionally, business communicates the historic results – lavishly so if they are good – while, prestigious projects apart, staying silent on present difficulties and future plans.

There are obvious commercial reasons, as well as the legal restrictions on disclosure, for discretion, but the workforce and the shareholders are interested in the way ahead, not the past. Raising enthusiasm and support for the programme is an important aim of internal communication and none are better to do the job than the directors.

The state of affairs may and should be clear to top executives but that is not the case with everyone else and simple presentations, discussion with the operating units, do much to raise morale and build the team.

It is all too common for the quarterly and half-year financial summaries or the commentaries issued to the markets and shareholders not to reach the factory floor. The employees are evidently not as important as the investing public or, worse, not thought to be interested in the results of their work. It is not the atmosphere in which success is built.

Failure to reach and make contact with the customer has an obvious and direct effect; poor internal communication also carries a price, in demotivation and disinterest. The network exploits the desire, the need people have to be involved, and the directors make it their business to carry out an annual programme of visits and formal presentations.

Casual calls may be perceived by the visiting dignitary to be good public relations, but in reality, condescension gives offence. The directors have a clear duty to communicate directly with their people.

THE COMMUNICATION HEALTH INDEX

The finances of the corporation are audited, production is reviewed by experts, marketing results measured by research – the effectiveness of communication is equally open to objective scrutiny. Is data being collected efficiently and distributed to maximum benefit? Is each internal 'customer' satisfied that the available information is adequate and allows maximum operational efficiency?

The chief executive and directors

The chief executive looks ahead to build for future change and must question, perhaps with the help of consultants, whether the corporation has the capacity to assess trends and build models of the changing universe. The function of the audit at this level is to query the validity of what is currently regarded as long-range planning.

The 'where are we going?' question has to be posed in each planning cycle and considered by the executive committee and the board. Periodically outside views will be sought to assess and comment on in-house thinking.

Operational data

The first audit task is to check **awareness** in the operating units of the data already available, both that generated internally and that to be found externally via the terminals. This is not a burdensome process, it is simply a review during each unit's planning cycle of what is being used of the material already available in-house.

The listings of the data available are continuously updated on the central information database but a verbal review is useful. Awareness can falter and the routine study of computer listings overlooked. For instance, a check of the market research programme company-wide may reveal work being undertaken by one office that is also of interest elsewhere – meanwhile, in the pressure of current work, the database listing has been forgotten.

Externally, the scope of the world databases is expanding continually, to the extent that grasp of the subject has become a specialist librarian skill. Knowing what is available, the base and validity of the contents, the commercial and technical conditions for connection, all have to be understood and manipulated to best advantage.

The audit of the external data includes examination of the **relevance** of the material being bought, its assessment against other sources and a check against duplication of purchase across the corporation. Data acquisition requires the same control as any other purchase.

Examined in parallel is the efficiency of the **software and the systems** being used to capture, download, analyse and study the data. As with the financial audit, such checking is all very obvious – but is it being done?

Undertaking the professional audit of the electronic network is an emerging concept. The use of outside expertise to study an existing set-up as opposed to writing more software, new systems, has yet to be generally accepted. Managements believe in the internal capacity and do not realize the need for, or the potential benefits of, an audit but the idea is gaining ground. Often it is introduced in tandem with a review of systems security.

Meetings

Meetings are a hidden cost. People are not budgeted by time allocation and no budget 'pays' for late starts, inadequate preparation or poor control. One 'style', a mark of the company in danger, is that of the meeting syndrome, when everyone from the president to the delivery van supervisor appears to be permanently locked 'in conference'.

By definition, meetings are a pooling of experience and information to arrive at conclusions and decisions. There has to be a question as to what can be contributed by people who spend most of their time at meetings – who is left minding the shop? It is not infrequent to hear an occasion described as having been 'a waste of everyone's time'.

I was once urgently invited across the Atlantic by a company proud of its structured planning, to advise on a marketing programme. On arrival I was told that the initial discussion had been fixed as the last of six 'conferences' in which the immediate host was scheduled to participate that day.

Having no intention of burdening anyone at the end of such a programme, the meeting was postponed to the following morning, for lunch to be taken out of another busy round. Returning in the early afternoon, we were both astonished: the host's office no longer existed, the partitioning had been re-arranged and the secretary re-assigned. The marketing function had been reorganized and my host no longer had a job. Not much later, the company, an honoured world name, went bankrupt – it was PanAm.

Some companies realize the problem – the Xerox Corporation is reported to ban meetings unless 'profitability outweighs cost' and helps the process by having all chairs removed after a fixed time from such occasions as do occur.

The audit problem lies in assessing meeting 'profitability'.

Certain gatherings, from board meetings to production scheduling, are inherent to organization. The function of the audit is to have a disinterested executive run a check on a given cycle of meetings and ask such questions as:

- whether any concerned a task that is in fact the responsibility of one desk;
- how many gatherings are necessary for a given purpose;
- how well each occasion was planned and managed – judged worth while by the participants;
- what the outcome was and how the result was communicated;
- in retrospect, what was finally achieved 'on the ground'?

The result is incorporated in the Communication Health Index (fully described in Chapter 11).

The print media

Assessing the value and direction of in-house publications is another audit task. The journals and newsletters must not be allowed to degenerate into the banal and routine. Management satisfaction with the magazines may not be shared by the target readership. One measure of interest and value lines in the level of voluntary contribution from the readers, by way of news reports, articles on achievements and activities, and also in the use made of the query and answer column.

The definitive measure of satisfaction, however, is to run a professionally monitored poll, to establish the effectiveness of what is being done and also to ask for improvements. Such a step represents only a small proportion of the costs of the publications but helps ensure that the expenditure and effort is worthwhile.

SUMMARY

The electronic systems, the written reports and print media, the consultative groups and the annual round of meetings, visits and contacts are the main physical links of the communication network.

Data input is geared to achievement of objectives, specifically to the budgets, by the direct linkage of all the workforce with the network. In particular, the planning process is pushed as far down the line as possible, aiming to tap all the talent available to the corporation.

The central desk helps assess the quality and availability of data in the network. The effectiveness and adequacy of each channel of communication is subject to audit in the construction of the Communication Health Index.

8

CHANGE AND EXTERNAL COMMUNICATION

External communication has to meet both marketing objectives and the challenge of change. Described here are the steps necessary to the building and maintenance of an efficient network.

INTRODUCTION

The management of external communication has two broad and inter-locking tasks:

- to keep the enterprise fully attuned to the **real** needs of the market, the client or customer, and on guard against benefits that are only assumed to exist by the supplier. The scope of this effort includes helping to identify current needs – and those that will be required tomorrow.
- To retain the **leadership of change**, to probe continuously into the 'area of the unknown'. Implied is the capacity to understand and absorb what is happening and the ability to utilize the intelligence effectively.

This concept of identifying and meeting need and providing service, is easy to postulate, to stress as being desirable and to set out as the corporate aim. It is, however, a difficult path to follow day after day, continuously at every level of contact. Genuinely staying 'close to the market', whether that is a collection of individual clients or a mass market, calls for the professional application of every tool of the communication function.

STAYING ATTUNED TO THE MARKET

Identification of the reality of market need is based on clear-headed study of the data fed into the network by managed communication. It is possible to be deluded by innovation, to rush into the market with the latest advance, full of understandable enthusiasm for what has been achieved. The customer, however, will see matters differently, and be less than thrilled. He or she has been asked to adapt and change, to invest in a purchase in the expection of solving a problem, meeting a need or improving efficiency, not to find only cosmetic if any change.

Adding more chrome may sell, but not against improved performance.

The development of information technology offers many examples. Horror stories abound of disasters that have followed seduction by technology to the exclusion of function or purpose. The tales continue. The sophisticated management of the London Stock Exchange had to write off millions and scrap a proposed dealing system, and this in the last decade of the twentieth century, by which time half the world has been operating computer systems for close on a generation.

The professional communicator is as likely to be fooled by his or her own jargon as anyone else. Typical is this letter (found at random) from a British national utility replying in the press to widespread criticism of certain practices:

> I would like to assure you that we continually endeavour to improve our standard of service and to take into account our customers' preferences and views. As part of our continuing commitment to the customer ...

i.e. they took the action that led to the complaints and mean to continue doing so while this suits the business and its methods.

The marketing textbook phraseology does not substitute for the identification of needs and 'commitment' to meeting them.

Development after the beginning

In the founding of a business, the successful entrepreneur instinctively gets it right. There is the idea, it is communicated and translated into action and a market is created, usually on the principle of having a better mousetrap for which the world will beat a path to the factory door. This happy situation does not last long and, in fact, the period before an even better mouse-elimination system appears is getting ever shorter. The imitative sometimes appear to have the best of market insight.

Meanwhile, if the fledgeling business is to grow, professional managers are brought in or, if not, history shows that the enterprise is soon in danger, at best unlikely to continue as an independent entity.

The entrepreneur often succeeds by exploiting a situation where the existing players have lost touch with their market. It can be a niche situation: capturing the switch to pool ahead of established billiards table manufacturers; exploiting new technologies distained by traditional manufacturers as the Japanese did with pianos; and then there was Steve Jobs, whose Macintosh and its mouse made the computer available to all (and then allowed others to forge ahead and benefit).

Change is also fundamental in the wider arena. The entire pattern of retail trading in Britain was altered by the entrepreneur who began selling white goods direct door-to-door in the 1960s. His actions shattered the established structure and led directly to the abolition of the infamous and archaic retail price maintenance system that had allowed manufacturers to fix retail prices by law.

While not obvious at the time, and it took another 25 years for the process to be generally accepted worldwide, that change in the UK was one of the first steps in the swing back to the freedom of the marketplace. The structure that had developed from the protectionism of the 1930s depression and the necessities of world war, was seen for what it was, the gross distortion of markets and trades, an enormous block to progress and higher living standards. The swing to the marketplace has gathered momentum ever since, to become accepted worldwide.

Meanwhile, the UK innovator failed to move with the times, respond to change and has long since been forgotten.

CAPTURING THE DATA

Capturing the data on the needs of the market and staying attuned to change requires continuous monitoring through every channel (Table 8.1).

Table 8.1 The market monitors

Direct contact	*Indirect monitor*
Working groups	Salespersons' reports
Consultative committees	Telephone and mail
Trade events	Market research
Meetings and conferences	Publications
Routine contact	

Direct contact

Working groups

Accepted as normal in, for instance, the construction industry, managed communication ensures that working groups are established to help guide all important projects. Actual or potential clients are invited to join the development team and to offer guidance on a continuing basis. Such groups are also of particular value to the service industries: the savings that could have been achieved, and the anguish that could have been avoided if this procedure had been followed by all software suppliers, are incalculable.

Mass market suppliers and manufacturers seek the same contact by setting up groups of consumers as representative as possible of the market. It is a specialist form of market research.

Consultative committees

Adapting existing services to meet the continuity of change is guided by consultative committees. No supplier, no matter how alert, has the hands-on day-to-day experience of their clients; their advice is needed. Since change is more often than not generated by competitive activity, the committees are important channels for the communication of what is happening 'out there in the field'.

The ultimate situation is to work on-site with the client, adapting and changing in the live situation. This level of experience also helps the supplier develop training programmes for both staff and new customers.

Trade events

The purpose of industry fairs and conventions is communication, the linking of suppliers, the industry and its market. Here is the opportunity to announce the latest developments and to study competitive change. Within the industry itself, these occasions often provide the opportunity for the annual meeting of the representative body and for the discussion of common difficulties.

The regular event can be something of a jamboree, to be enjoyed and then forgotten except as a source of folklore. That accepted, managed communication also requires a return, in the form of data and intelligence. Essential discipline is the attendance report, which notes the theme or display of participants and technological and market developments. Also to be covered are the activities of the trade body and any intelligence gleaned, particularly on the movement of people and the situation of competitors, during casual or social contact.

There is often unsuspected interest in a given point among colleagues who have not attended so that the report, perhaps in summary form, needs to be well circulated. It is also noted in the electronic mail, allowing anyone with a particular interest to enquire further. Finally, events are reported in the magazines and newsletters – nothing is allowed to be 'lost'.

Meetings and conferences

Attendance at external gatherings is usually for defined commercial or technological reasons, in the area of direct responsibility of the participants. Consequently, it is common for these events not to be reported 'back home'. The delegate will return over the weekend and then on the Monday, put it to the back of his or her mind while dealing with the accumulation on their desk.

Meanwhile, the product managers and operational teams, the advertising agency and perhaps research and development will not be informed or become aware of a development, the significance of which only they might recognize. When the business is hit by the competitive development, six months or a year later, the effect will be more severe and reaction more difficult than need have been the case.

Managed communication requires that conference attendance is recorded by a full report and that it is noted over the electronic network and in the company publications.

Routine contact

Keeping close to the client, maintaining good relationships and staying in touch generally are matters of personal satisfaction, even of pride at every level. Some managers who have little direct contact with the market may gain valuable intelligence from their meetings with colleagues in the industry. In any event, being personally 'in touch' is not enough: the company-wide communication environment requires that all data is recorded in the relevant product, competitive or industry database.

Many corporations place emphasis on having their senior people in touch with top management of client organizations, even where these contacts are removed from the actual business situation. It is not always easy to apply the rules but senior executives must also be made conscious of their responsibility for updating the data on the central files.

Important intelligence on competitors and technology can emerge during social contact at senior levels. Everyone likes to be in the know and to be seen as market knowledgeable, but intelligence is of limited value if not made available to the corporation as a whole. The director in charge of communication has a delicate task at peer level to persuade his or her colleagues to cooperate in the network.

Indirect monitors

Salespersons' reports

There is not a successful salesperson who does not believe that he or she adds an intangible plus, a personality extra to the task. These contacts are those of individuals as people, not simply as a conduit between two organizations, and it is here that much intelligence is to be found.

Managed communications captures this data for the network. Whatever the routine of sales reporting, there is provision, perhaps on the forms or by prompting on the terminal, for the recording of data additional to the routine. Comment is called for on the market activity of competitors, on terms of trade, on product improvements and relevant people news. The system does have two requirements, that the sales people are trained in what and how to report and that there is an incentive. Good and relevant reporting deserves recognition and direct reward.

Telephone and mail

The system handles every comment and complaint, whether voiced over the telephone, in writing or brought in by a salesperson. Apart from being 'handled' in the sense of dealing with the matter, each point is recorded in a dossier or database product service file. A procedure is required to ensure first that the data is captured and then that the entries are in standard format and as complete as possible. Some form of check ensures complete recording. Repeated entry of the same point may not be thought necessary by an assistant but it is this very frequency of mention that is important in product assessment.

Urgent problems will attract immediate attention but each dossier is also subjected to a formal periodic review, most conveniently early on in the planning cycle. The data combines with market research findings to give the enterprise a powerful tool in the continuing struggle for market leadership.

The shop floor

Great value is lost if the daily flow of data is not captured systematically. The remarks on packaging by a shop assistant, the product comments heard on the showroom floor by the sales assistants, perhaps not remarkable in themselves, when combined in a product file highlight negative features, warn of potential difficulties and indicate opportunities. With this information on readily accessible file, the planning process is given a promising and confident start. Meanwhile, the frontline staff see themselves as an integral element of the team and feel encouraged to contribute and help build the business.

The 'hot line' to management, whether in the form of a return or through the terminal, becomes a feature and adds interest to the routine of the working day. Recording must be simple and no burden, particularly for employees working on commission. The system works best when linked to some form of recognition and tangible reward.

Market research

Data on sales, usually available from independent, professional agencies and becoming ever more sophisticated and timely, guides much of enterprise. This is particularly the case in the mass markets and no manufacturer of, for example, groceries, drink or pharmaceuticals can operate effectively unless subscribing to, and having the capacity to use, these market statistics.

In parallel to this quantitative counting of units moving through the checkouts, out of the showroom, another form of market research, the 'qualitative', studies the reasons for behaviour – the motivations and preferences of the consumer. In the main, such studies are arranged by a company anxious for information on a particular product area or market segment. It may be thought necessary to confirm in-house views or to study new aspects on which there is no data. In any event, market research is a major tool, necessary in the continuing struggle to keep operations aligned to the market.

Market research is a professional tool for drawing the difficult dividing line between inspired hunch and disastrous fixation. It is not unknown for a senior person to form a view, perhaps one based on a random contact, that is out of line with corporate data. There are no guarantees as to what might be right but careful market research will at least help in arriving at a measured decision.

Publications

Managed communication provides for the routine and systematic monitoring of specialist and industry publications. It can be a task for the central desk. Specific material is circulated direct to the relevant office or manager. More generally, topics are reported in the magazines and also noted on the central databases, perhaps on the product files or in the record of technological change.

MANAGING CHANGE

Managing change through the concept of giving service, of continually staying abreast of the market, implies three functions for external communication:

- the **achievement of sales**, building revenue by the marketing effort;
- creation of and safeguarding an **image**, one of giving satisfaction, of being ahead technically and yet being seen as responsible and careful;
- and, in parallel, **capturing the data** necessary for the achievement of these objectives.

Communication with the outside has to overcome a special hurdle. Whereas the internal audience cares and is anxious to be kept informed, the external world is entirely oblivious and has to be offered incentive even to listen, never mind respond. Communication with the market has first to break through this indifference and then be heard against all the 'noise' of the marketplace.

Market-stall traders shouting their wares adjust the message each day to the demands and temper of the crowds. They at least have the advantage of calling out to people who have come to market expecting to listen and possibly be open to conviction.

In the wider world environment, all are subjected to a daily stream of messages, first as mass-market consumers but also as individual clients for professional and technical services. In the event, we only listen to what interests us or promises some benefit. News of what the supplier is doing, of his or her situation is entirely ignorable.

Richard Branson, the successful British entrepreneur, puts it this way:

> The fact that some people have supplied a particular line of products for years is not an indication of excellence. It is much more likely an indication of neglect.

His method is to experiment endlessly with new methods, products and market approaches. He also believes that small units are better at staying close to the market and managing to keep up with change. Each of the Virgin businesses was set up by him to run as an independent operation, managed by the staff, and a large network was swiftly established.

The same philosophy has been applied at the other end of the industrial spectrum, by the engineering giant, Asea Brown Boveri. Certain that there is no protection from the storms of change, even for the most powerful, Percy Barnevik, the managing director, has forcefully applied a policy of empowerment since taking over in Sweden. Believing that only small, dedicated units can have the flexibility of communication to keep pace with change he has drastically restructured every one of a series of major acquisitions.

The 2000-strong head office of the original Asea was quickly cut to one of 200; the 1600 in the Mannheim centre became 100. The major merger with Brown Boveri in 1987 saw a 4000-strong centre cut to 200. Instead, a legion of autonomous profit centres is supervised by a small team of executives who include 60 or so managers of the different areas of business.

The main task of these managers is to communicate, to pass information between units, to capture competitive data and compare costs and performance. This is done from offices ranging in size from one to a dozen people.

The structure is completed by having the areas-of-business offices report to an executive committee of a dozen, giving a giant world corporation with a complex mix of businesses just three layers of management.

Barnevik believes a unit becomes a business when linked directly to the customer, that everything is changed by having the buyer face you at a desk or talking on the end of the telephone. It is lack of flexibility, the inability to respond to change, that will destroy corporate giants.

The results of the change for people was also interesting: about a third went in natural wastage, a similar proportion found themselves line jobs but the other third moved into peripheral activities, setting up independent units and competing for business from ABB and elsewhere, at market prices.

Direct response to market change

One approach to flexibility is to identify on a regular basis, perhaps each quarter, the two or three features or procedures that are least satisfactory and which come closest to 'driving the customer mad'. Analyses of these situations, the allocation of specific responsibility for each improvement and subsequent review of results achieved, help keep the market in focus.

Reporting the outcome through the network, in the magazines, on the databases and at meetings, encourages emulation and equivalent response from other units and offices.

The in-house electronic network is also used to warn the frontline staff dealing with the customer of current difficulties. One example is the way employees of major utilities are alerted to actual and possible problems and put into a position of being able to respond directly to queries. With a watermain burst or an electricity cut, the central desks are able to say what is happening and, most importantly, are able to reassure that the matter is known and in hand.

Built into a current-problem monitor are all outstanding points, which remain on display to the 'end', that is until resolved or consciously abandoned for explained reasons. Sales people and travelling executives can update themselves on outstanding issues at the start of the working day, and are able to answer customer queries on the status of an order, the outcome of an unusual instruction.

A corollary is the continued reminder by way of prompting all users of the data of their responsibilities for recording and capturing the information that comes to hand within their operational ambience. Cooperation is assisted where the input procedures are simple and clearly set out on the terminals. Data capture should be an agenda item for all routine meetings and be featured in the publications, as well as prompted on the screens.

Maverick thinking

Managed communication encourages lateral thinking across organizational lines and allows people to browse and express their thoughts and ideas.

The 'why don't we have ...?' type of question can be posed without embarrassment through a recognized procedure, in the electronic mail or perhaps via the central desk. Either as a result of their own experience or from customer comment, employees may wonder why the product range is limited, does not incorporate desirable features or has been allowed to become dated.

Little of all this will be 'new' but, given a live network, it is a simple task to answer suggestions. Perhaps the idea was tried in the past or there are technical difficulties not immediately obvious or there has been a conscious decision to invest available resources elsewhere. Nevertheless, the environment remains one of questioning and searching for improvement.

In cases judged worth further investigation, the originator is involved, even if only peripherally where the activity is outside the immediate area of responsibility. Suggestions found to be worth while and adopted are, of course, recognized and rewarded.

COMMUNICATION WITH SUPPLIERS

Strong links with suppliers are a feature of managed communication. The obvious foundation is an accurate, updated record of suppliers, their standing and capabilities. A central record or database may reveal some overlap of supply but this can be desirable as a guarantee of continuity and of quality. The monitor assures that the position is known, that it is not wasteful but based on conscious decision.

A corollary is to maintain awareness of alternatives, at least for key supplies. In case of difficulty, even disaster, there might be no time to research sources and all data relevant to saving the situation needs to be to hand. Managed communication ensures that the dangers inherent in supply are considered, reviewed periodically and records are maintained, perhaps on a central database, of alternative sources or methods.

The need for such a monitor of supplier links has been highlighted in a critical report on the relationship between UK car manufacturers and their suppliers. The author, Prof. Richard Lamming of Bath University School of Management, noting that many practices adopted to improve communication had failed, went on to report:

> The mistrust which is in evidence is the result of many years of broken promises, abuse of confidence and general acrimony in the industry ... in developing new working agreements with their suppliers most vehicle manufacturers still appear to deal more in rhetoric than reality.[1]

The same link is needed between the suppliers of services and their clients. Following much criticism, the Bank of England conducted an inquiry into charges that small businesses were not being treated fairly by the major clearing banks. The finding was that the only serious criticism of the banks was their poor communication with these customers.

Suppliers are also important sources of intelligence. Every supplier is by definition in touch with the industry and the competition. Corporate buyers, keen and trained operators in their field, are in a good position to capture data from the trade. They can be encouraged to do so by being made aware of what is required and by having a simple routine for reporting on each contact. The material can be handled by the central desk.

Suppliers can also be useful as monitors of internal procedures. It is not unknown for two departments of a company not to be 'speaking' and issuing separate and conflicting instructions to outside suppliers. Objective study of the supplier viewpoint, perhaps undertaken periodically through market research professionals, can reveal expensive organizational gaps and personnel difficulties. Such studies can also point to opportunities for procedural and communication improvements.

RECRUITING WITH CARE

Recruitment methods are a channel of external communication and for projecting an image. There are the obvious criteria, now generally a matter of law, as regards sex and race bias in the advertising and job descriptions. Increasingly, too, the question of age discrimination, already illegal in the USA , is becoming an issue in Europe.

However, one area likely to be overlooked is the treatment of rejected applicants. Even in good times, when application numbers can be small, not everyone may be interviewed; during the years of recession, hundreds of job applicants will not be seen, left to feel that they have been given no opportunity of putting their case.

The reasons for non-selection will vary: many applicants cannot prepare a CV or are applying for the wrong job, whether over-, under- or non-qualified.

There is also the physical difficulty of dealing with hundreds if not thousands of letters and responses. It is this very volume of contact, however, that suggests care and the realization that all these people are consumers and have families. Some will doubtless become influential.

The managed communication environment ensures:

- Job advertising is as clear as the law allows. A little imagination can hint that youthful fitness or specific experience is considered essential, cutting down on application numbers, attracting the 'right' people.
- Every applicant gets a reply. Job seekers are often emotionally vulnerable and may long harbour a feeling of resentment at apparently having been ignored.
- Replies are very carefully crafted. Specifically avoided is the negative option letter: 'If you do not hear from us by — your application will have failed.' All rejection is difficult but it can be handled better than that and some hint of personal concern and attention softens the blow.

In every group of applicants, even for the lower jobs, there will be car owners, insurance buyers and householders. Alienation of even a handful of, say, car buyers, carries a hidden and possibly continuing cost, well in excess of providing a little extra care with recruitment communication.

Outside skills and resources

The resources database becomes increasingly important as functions are contracted out and operating units concentrate on core activity. It is also an insurance against disaster.

An example would be the illness or departure of a key executive at a critical time, possibly in an important branch. There is no manager available to step in and keep matters under control until a replacement of suitable calibre can be found, and that may be a matter of months. Perhaps an operation is going badly and the responsible management seems unable to cope.

A possibility in these circumstances is crisis management, the temporary employment of a qualified outside executive. It can be a known individual or a manager made available through the specialist agencies and consultancies. In the circumstances there is no time and perhaps no resource to start investigations of the background of suitable individuals and the reputation and status of agencies, and a reasonably maintained file then comes into its own.

More generally, there is occasional need for expertise such as cannot be available in-house on a permanent basis. There is a call for a statistician, a specialist engineer, a designer or a materials expert. It is a communication function to maintain a corporation-wide list of experts who are known and have been used in the past.

In parallel is the record of requirements and of outside expertise regularly employed. A central source of information on all consultants and outside experts will, for instance, show if operating units are paying retainer fees to different people for the same purpose or, alternatively, will reveal a resource that someone has been unable to find.

A multinational may well decide that for political reasons, overlapping consultants are desirable. A central record ensures that the facts are known, that costs can be measured against value received. Management is also put into the position of being able to meet calls for help and to volunteer expertise when problems surface.

SUMMARY

External communication encompasses both the function of staying attuned to the market and of managing change. It is dependent on the systematic capture of all available data.

The market is monitored by direct contacts, ranging from consultative working groups through to the industry convention, and from indirect sources, including reports, market research and technical publications.

Staff cooperation in the capture of data is encouraged by installing routines, and by a system of recognition and reward. Maverick thinking is encouraged.

The responsibilities of external communication include maintaining strong links with suppliers, the sensitive handling of recruitment and keeping an updated record of available expertise.

REFERENCES

1. Lamming, R. (1994) *Relationships between Vehicle Manufacturers and Suppliers*, Department of Trade and Industry.

9

INTERNATIONAL COMMUNICATION

It is easier to know man in general than to understand one man in particular (La Rochefoucauld).

Generalizations on markets and people are commonplace, the skill is in communication with the individual. Meeting the challenge of worldwide communication means exploring, understanding and then successfully exploiting cultural mores and patterns. For the professional, 'abroad' and 'out there' do not exist. The reality is a segmented marketplace, to be won piece by piece.

INTRODUCTION

Effective world communication is based on:

- an attitude, developing an open mind to the distant, the different and unknown;
- understanding and accepting that there is no 'abroad', no anonymous 'them';
- sensitivity to varying perceptions and behaviour patterns.

The principles of communication apply equally in one country, a dozen, or to the world market. The approach will be tailored to the different perceptions and customs of each, the media mix will vary, but given this care the communication network operates fully and effectively.

There is, then, no 'abroad' and no 'them out there' but market segments made up of recognizable individuals. Gaining understanding of, and then successfully exploiting, their cultural mores and behaviour patterns is the challenge.

RECOGNIZING AND WORKING WITH THE DIFFERENCES

Effective international communication, whether undertaken by the individual or as part of a corporate network, is achieved by avoiding assumptions and generalizations. The function is built on an understanding of and sensitivity to the manners, habits and culture of each market.

An individual executive is aware of the barriers to communication in the home society. In adapting to the world view, it takes a conscious effort to remember that such difficulties exist elsewhere and demand the same degree of concentration, market knowledge and insight. 'They' are as sophisticated as 'we', whether peasants in India or remote fishermen in Norway. The inhabitants of each country are as segmented as 'ours'.

Language

The impact of the visual continues to grow but language is and will remain the basic medium of communication. Although there has been a steep decline in the number, it is thought that there are still perhaps 10 000 separate tongues spoken in the world.

The business communicator will not be involved with more than a handful of them but nevertheless faces difficulties. The most obvious is that some markets are officially bilingual, notably Belgium and Canada. Switzerland has four official languages (and, in contrast to almost universal practice, packaging and instructions often carry no English version).

In these markets, the lingual divisions are geographic but countries can also be multilingual nationally. The younger generation in one of the world's poorer countries, Tanzania, now uses three languages – the tribal (these have a wide etymology and are not dialects), the lingua franca of Swahili, which is a legacy of the Arab period, and English, the medium of education.

Many if not most markets have minority tongues, such as Welsh in Britain, Catalan in Spain, Spanish in the US, which all have marketing importance. Increasingly, governments and local media cater for immigrant communities, notably Spanish in the USA but there is Turkish in Germany and Hindu and Urdu in the UK.

English has become the predominant language, specifically for commerce and technology, but this global spread has produced its own forms of diversity and dissipation. Speakers of the language from, say, Jamaica will not be understood in the inner city areas of Glasgow. Misunderstanding can result from believing that 'the Americans', 'the Australians' and 'the British' will have an equal grasp of what is said, of a message.

A Londoner has only to read the American writer Thomas Pynchon to realize there is a basis of truth in the old joke of being 'divided by a common language', in the meaning of words and expressions and also in thoughts and lifestyle. Meanings are continually altering and new colloquialisms are being adopted.

The user of English is well advised to be circumspect. In some markets, notably France, there can be resistance to and even resentment of the automatic use of English. Neither does education guarantee understanding. Iran under the Shah had perhaps the highest proportion of English-educated executives and technicians in the whole region, a fact that has not prevented the total breakdown of communication with the West.

The second great transplanted European tongue, Spanish, is not displaying the tendency to dissipate to quite the same degree, but Arabic and Chinese, two other languages spoken across important national boundaries, do demand care when used by non-natives.

Habits and customs

It becomes a matter of great personal satisfaction to feel at home in different cultures, to establish confidence and rapport, to make friends with colleagues and customers.

The novice traveller can be misled by the natural politeness of hosts, by the euphoria of the novel and strange, into believing that he or she has 'arrived' and is accepted. A little experience will bring disillusionment and realization that there is indeed much to learn.

It can come as a shock for the European or American interlocator to realize, perhaps some time into or even after a contact, that the smiling 'yes' meant 'yes, I have understood' or 'yes, thank you for explaining' but most certainly not 'yes, I agree – let us go ahead'. In Japan and other markets too, it is not done to offend a visitor by a 'no'. Even when a proposal is clearly attractive, the Japanese will want to take time to reflect and consult the whole group.

Many societies place considerable emphasis on personal relationships. A Japanese customer will want to evaluate the individual as well as the corporation. Once there is agreement, it is anticipated that the relationship will be long-lasting and the parties will be loyal to each other. In Japan relationships can be planned not only in years but built over generations. A business will employ among a new intake members of families important in adjacent sectors, perhaps as specialist suppliers or leading customers. These recruits may take years to reach positions of importance but their presence in the company is proof of the integrity and stability of the business, the understanding and correctness of attitude of the principals.

The negotiation stance

There is irony in having politeness inhibit communication. Correct behaviour in many societies includes the avoidance of disagreement with a visitor, to seek the expression of views that it is thought he or she wishes to hear. This is a characteristic of some of the peoples of Africa but is also to be found in polite circles in Mediterranean countries.

In Spain, a conversation may well have to be prolonged or resumed after a break before the host will feel him- or herself in a position to bring forward and express the problems and difficulties of the situation. In fact, the real reasons may never surface: if the proposal has no interest, the host will wish to avoid distress and simply allow matters to fade away in delay and polite vagueness.

The handling of negotiations varies. In the offices of a Muslim, the expectation can be for a period of small talk with business long delayed, perhaps to the last half hour of the time available. Many Chinese will seek to build contact by expressing interest in the personal – enquiring about families or possible mutual interests – before starting to consider the matter in hand.

The opposite is usually true in Germany. Here reluctance to get down to business, to extend preliminary remarks for more than a minute or two, is taken as a sign of lack of interest.

A visitor needs to be forewarned!

Personal behaviour

One of the more difficult areas of international communication lies in the mores governing physical contact. At its simplest, this means learning when and how to shake hands, on every occasion, as in France, rarely (outside the international set) with some of the peoples of India. Many Americans expect a 'firm' handshake, a greeting that is not so well appreciated in Latin Europe.

Touching among men when meeting and leaving, whether the hand on the shoulder or the full hug, varies widely; gesturing with the hands or the manner of sitting, all play a role in gaining acceptance. Socially, the kissing habit can be confusing. In France, greeting the hostess varies by region: two pecks, one on each cheek, in Paris; four in the Western areas of the country.

Stereotyping

A great barrier to effective communication is stereotyping – unthinkingly applying a prejudice to a country or people. It is a trait to be faced honestly. Not every Nigerian man of affairs is corrupt; most British and French partners find that they can trust each other as well as anyone; doing business with Arabs can be harmonious.

Surveys of attitudes among executives often reveal the historic stereotypes – the Germans are seen by the British to be efficient, hardworking but lacking humour and flexibility. The Italians have a low perspective of Spanish management capability and the view from Spain is not much different. The French do not place much trust in the British, and so on worldwide.

Unfortunately, preconceptions and prejudices are commonplace; it may require much strength of mind in the middle of a tiring tour, on a hot day, not to have judgment clouded by the stereotype. In the end, it is a matter of personal discipline and of training. The alert communicator knows him- or herself and understands these moods for what they are, to be put firmly aside. It helps not to express such views, nor to acquiesce in their expression by colleagues, at any time, to concentrate thought on the individual and not on 'them'.

Politeness

Despite all the differences, genuine politeness is recognized everywhere. Mistakes of behaviour, in ways of eating, or with permitted forms of expression, will not give offence, but be seen for what they are, provided the visitor shows respect and is interested in the hosts.

True politeness, however, is shown by the visitor who has taken the trouble to prepare in advance and has given forethought to the visit.

It would be a serious mistake, for instance, to arrive in Japan without visiting cards. It is *de rigueur* for these to be exchanged at every contact. It would also be expected of the visitor to arrive with a plentiful supply of brochures and pamphlets describing his corporation. Since they expect a relationship to be permanent, the Japanese are avid collectors of background data and it is an extra politeness for the material to have at least a summary insert in Japanese.

It helps, as in all societies, to have an introduction, either in writing or verbally and, in Japan at least, to keep strictly to the appointment – it shows respect for the host's time.

Of prime importance is an understanding of negotiating practice. In Europe, one usually talks directly with the responsible executive. In Japan, however, contact might start by meeting the president but that would be for the sake of politeness, not to discuss business. The actual negotiating will be with (a team of) middle management. The expectation will be for low-key moderate discussion, not for them the hard-hitting, forceful presentation that is the norm in a US office.

Difficulties with the infrastructure

In much of the world, the infrastructure is poor and facilities taken for granted in the West are scarce or nonexistent. Without forewarning and adequate preparation, not least coming in the right frame of mind, the traveller will at best experience frustrations and at worst fail to achieve any purpose.

Preparation is particularly important for the expatriate being posted 'abroad'. Many of those moving into East Europe since the collapse of the Soviet empire, for instance, have found their expectations, or those of their employer, to be unrealistically optimistic. There are endless hurdles to registration, arranging offices or gaining access to services of every kind, and the mechanics of living in general can turn first plans into nightmares. The structures and culture imposed on three generations by communism are taking time to change, a process hampered further by crime, lawlessness and political instability.

None of this is new. Similar conditions have long since been faced in Africa and elsewhere in the developing world. In earlier times, the slower pace and the sharing of experience with compatriots allowed the newcomer to adapt. Today's executive is faced with an urgency for results and achievements.

In this climate, the communication network becomes an important tool for successful expansion. It helps first by having accessible on the databases all the intelligence on the market accumulated internally and available from external sources. Trade departments, consulates and specialists and their publications offer intelligence invaluable to the novice and even of help to the more experienced. The network, perhaps through the central desk, must have the capacity to capture, edit and enter the material for ready access through the terminals.

Second, the network terminal gives the expatriate live contact with the resources back home. Without backing and contact, the individual working in isolation can lose a sense of proportion and be over-whelmed by difficulties that would be seen as trivial in normal circumstances. It is also comforting to be kept in touch with corporate affairs generally, to feel reassured that one is not forgotten and that career prospects are not being diminished by absence from the centre.

MANAGING THE INTERNATIONAL NETWORK

Management of international communication recognizes the importance both of the personal characteristics that are essential to the individual and of the support that is required of the organization (Table 9.1).

Table 9.1 The elements of a world communication network

Areas of personal sensitivity	Factual data on corporate structure
Language	Recruitment and training
Habits and customs	Social database
Behaviour	Market database
Politeness	Reporting structure
Stereotyping	Meetings and conferences
	Visiting schedules

The international communicator recognizes no 'home' country. A head office exists and regional centres may be responsible for groups of markets but each unit is an entity in which the experienced executive can operate with confidence. Organization has to adapt to the ever-changing world market; currently the growth of economic blocs, in Europe, Latin and North America and perhaps in the Pacific, is being matched by altered management structures.

One system is to have teams located at a central office managing a category of products or services for perhaps all Europe, treating the continent as one market. Another structure is to retain the set-up by country but to allocate continent-wide responsibility for coordination and development of product categories to given offices, e.g. Madrid might oversee Brand A and Brussels Brand B in addition to running the country budgets. In practice there are probably as many variations in organizations as there are multinationals but the principles of product and budget responsibility are common at all.

Common features and differences

International organizations have the advantage of a corporate culture and standard routines for doing business and conducting affairs and of running common services or products in the markets. Executives usually have similar social and educational backgrounds and have travelled, if not studied and worked, outside their home countries. Over the years, friendships are formed and a personal network has been established.

Nevertheless, differences remain and approaches to business vary. For instance, it is unusual for the German budget to be anything other than a large package, complete in every detail, whereas the French manager will arrive with a slim document, some of it probably handwritten at the last moment. It will often contain a table or two of statistics and a theoretical, intellectual analysis which is virtually incomprehensible to colleagues.

The British will be somewhere in between, possibly taking a broader brush to more uncertain points. The American manager has normally followed the policy manual format to the letter but striven for the unusual by way of a deal.

World corporations range from those run by a unified management to organizations of several divisions, each global in its own right. The common features will include:

- head office coordination, if only of the budgets; it is usual also to have some form of central communication, if only for newsletters and announcements;
- a formal reporting structure;
- an annual cycle of meetings and visiting;
- a staff policy, which also covers training and the search for talent.

In the managed communication environment, the network runs familiarization programmes, commonly in the form of seminars and backed by self-training videos, and a database of the corporate experience of each market. This should also include hints of the 'do's and 'don't's by market.

The facilities for cross-border familiarization within Europe and between Europe and the USA, at universities, through specialist courses and continuing programmes, is extensive. The scope elsewhere is also expanding. One interesting example is the programme funded by the European Union and the Japanese Ministry for International Trade and Industry under which senior European executives are sent to Japan to familiarize themselves with business practices and related cultural behaviour. This course is designed both for managers of companies trading with Japan, or acting as contractors to Japanese enterprises abroad, and also for executives who may be moved to Japan by a European concern.

Recruitment and training

Recruiting 'foreign' management, training executives for overseas appointment, is a specialist area of communication. Even given in-house expertise, conditions vary so much that consultants are widely used.

For example, in Germany it is the candidate who is often expected to specify salary expectations while in the USA and Britain, the figures are spelt out in the advertisement, usually with the fringe benefits that establish the status and position of the post. A German employer will set this out in the advertisement together with the precise qualifications required – and there is no point in applying if one does not have them.

A German company is unlikely to appoint a manager from outside the industry whereas this is not unusual in the UK or the USA.

French employers are also reticent about setting out terms and benefits and in the end these may be more aligned to the individual and his or her qualifications than to the actual post. This procedure reflects the more exact requirements of the employer, particularly if the product of a *grande école* is sought; the emphasis is on the intellect rather than the 'drive' and 'enthusiasm' often quoted by Anglo-Saxon employers. In France, status comes from intellectual achievement; managers are expected to be analytical and to work on the basis of analysis, not on the hunch or by adaptation, traits admired in other countries.

Interviewing

Interviews between people of different backgrounds carry the seeds of misunderstanding. The acceptable way of opening a conversation, the degree and frequency of eye contact and the level of jocularity are all among the imponderables of personal contact that are multiplied by cultural diversity.

Breaking the ice, usually with a comment on the weather, is common in Britain but can indicate lack of interest or uncertainty in Arab countries (where the stable weather understandably does not hold the same fascination). In China there might be seemingly intrusive questions about the family, such as would not be addressed to a stranger in Europe.

Individual behaviour apart, there are many cultural subtleties. A listener who makes continuous eye contact appears obtrusive, even rude, to many Africans; in contrast, someone who looks away or elsewhere while listening will be considered inattentive by a European.

International operations need executives to be familiar with these pitfalls. The more the global market is integrated – and two score countries have been added since the collapse of communism – the more complex the task facing the world business and its managers.

Exchange of experience

One strength of the multinationals, the diversity of thinking and approach among the employees, is exploited to the full by the communication network. A problem in one area can, through the planning procedure, the central desk, the database of available expertise, benefit from the experience of, or solution found elsewhere. A success in one market will be published for the benefit of all and ideas and new developments are made known worldwide.

This is equally true of costs. Each line of expenditure, from production to sales support, is compared between markets in the search for economy.

At the same time, a measure of the team spirit is the willingness to help. Perhaps an office will lend expertise to assist a colleague through a bad patch, and continue to carry the expense. In contrast, poor morale is indicated by endless arguments, often set out in angry memos that are widely copied, on such subjects as internal cost allocations. Communication is poor when senior management wastes time by having to rule on the credit or debit of a particular item.

The personnel offices

Close links between the personnel offices is a feature of managed communication. Conditions of employment, both statutory and customary, vary widely, as do the costs of the elements of the compensation package, of pensions, vacations and health.

The provision of cars is a case in point, common in the UK, relatively unusual in the USA, so prohibitively expensive in some markets as to allow but a small vehicle to the top manager. Clearly, common policies are not possible and the result is that personnel offices are seen as a purely local function, relegated to in-market administration.

In fact, close liaison between these offices, to the extent of an occasional world conference, forges an important link in the communication network. Apart from the technical (e.g. pension provisions), two important functions benefit – the incentives programme and training. The first is a matter of sharing experience and ideas but training will certainly be more developed in some markets than in others.

The pace of change, the demand for the continuous update of skills, is a strain on both the organization and the individual. It helps to share training expertise by the exchange of personnel and in the provision of materials. The single most common and perhaps most popular training mode is the conference or seminar but these occasions have the limitations of expense and are often broad-based. Instead, the concept of individual self-development is growing and it is in this area that the personnel departments can jointly set goals, recommend methods and produce materials.

Videos are a good example. These are relatively cheap, more so when produced centrally, and, given liaison, subjects can be allocated between offices: Tokyo might take on team-building; New York, sales techniques; Frankfurt, time management. It is also a responsibility of personnel offices to stay in touch with new techniques, such as guided learning and mentoring. Overall, the holder of the communication portfolio needs to ensure that the expertise is developed economically and then spread across the organization.

Specialists

Specialists have often to be 'shared' between operations, perhaps working in relative isolation on the allotted task and not linked directly to the communication network. It can happen for a specialist to arrive on a specific job, perhaps involving liaison with an outside supplier, without the local management being involved, or even informed. That is, unless something goes wrong, and then tempers tend to rise.

With managed communication, the specialists' programme, the results achieved and new development and improvements are reported through the network. It can be done in magazine articles and further discussed at management meetings. Details of the various schedules are also carried on the database, keeping the individual operations in touch with what is happening and what might be expected.

People contact

No matter how large or structured it may be, personal contact remains vital for the health of the corporation. People respond and work better with those they know than to the requirements of an anonymous memo.

Smaller offices, in particular, can feel isolated and develop a perception of being alone in struggling with problems of a unique complexity not understood at head office. An executive running a business in the Third World, or a small unit remote from the main operation, sees problems grow into hurdles, can become defeatist and let matters slide.

Travel costs may be relatively heavy but here communication through personal contact is particularly important. Only by getting away and viewing matters from the outside will a sense of perspective return and enthusiasm be maintained.

The annual cycle

The formal structure of personal contact will centre on the annual cycle. There are usually two formal gatherings, one for the presentation by each unit of its updated long-range plan and the second for the budget discussion. Here managers place the plans before a group made up of their peers and senior management.

The system ensures first that all available experience is brought to bear on each situation and also that ideas and innovations are spread across the company. Added value is given to these events by informal discussion, over meals and during the social events. It is then that personal links are forged and the foundation laid for the informal network by which so much is achieved.

Meetings and conferences

Internal meetings

A firm rule: no matter how advanced the conference centre and its facilities, an experienced convenor always runs through a personal checklist covering programme and arrangements. It is surprising the disruption that can result from a simple oversight, such as failure to provide storage for overcoats: people searching around, placing coats on window sills, under chairs or in odd corners on the floor, can get matters off to a poor start.

Constant interruption for calls and messages also distract and are unfair to the speaker of the moment. Secretarial facilities are a key requirement.

A realistically spaced agenda is important. Time is always at a premium and executives who have travelled halfway round the globe do not welcome having their contribution squeezed into a few minutes before lunch, held over to the end of a tiring day. Attendees at international meetings run disparate businesses, such as a single service in the US being larger than the total turnover in another country. The agenda will be arranged accordingly but should timings slip, contributions from the smaller units cannot be put aside and made irrelevant.

The language will usually be English but despite appearances of fluency, not all attendees will be equally comfortable. Presentations are difficult enough without an added barrier of language and, while simultaneous translation is normally out of the question, a chairman or convenor can help by pacing the delivery or summarizing key points. Individuals weak in the language can be seated next to more fluent colleagues for support.

A useful technique is for highlights to be recorded and copied to all for repeat listening at home. This arrangement has the added benefit of allowing managers on their return to bring the world stage to their in-market teams.

Another is to move international gatherings between major offices and, by having them attend, expose senior local personnel to the corporate-wide culture. Given the role and cost of international gatherings, it is helpful for the holder of the communication portfolio to have some form of coordinating role for the annual cycle. So much goes on, so many people are on the move, that someone should have an overview to help ensure that these expensive resources are being used to best advantage.

Conferences

International conferences and specialist symposia are an established feature of the annual round, essential to the progress of an industry, a profession or an area of expertise. Managed communication maximizes the benefits by:

- an event report, recording the attendance, important themes and the announcement of new developments;
- a listing of all contacts. This noting of personalities can be of crucial importance in an international corporation. A leading figure inaccessible at home, is available and receptive when seen at a global event and can subsequently by introduced to the in-market team.

Visiting and visitors

Visiting is continuous in the international environment. At one level, directors and senior executives call to 'show the flag', to be followed by the routine visiting of line managers and specialists, both to and from operations.

The key communication requirement is preparation, followed by preparation and preparation. Time is always short and preparation is required both of the visitor and the host. The former needs to study the background and suggest an agenda, allowing the host to gather necessary materials and make arrangements in good time. The visit can then be devoted to business and not frittered away in the mechanics of attempting to get things done at the last minute.

That said, contact between an operating manager and a top executive allows a broader brush review than might be the case in routine meetings with line management. Reporting structures cannot be subverted but there must be allowance for contact across the normal lines, for a lapse into the unorthodox.

The senior visitor brings excitement, sets out the corporate perspectives. In reverse, field managers are called to head office outside the annual routine, given the chance to meet the senior people, perhaps attend a special event such as an industry fair.

Again, the communication portfolio-holder is in a position to assess from the perspectives of the boardroom, the overall benefit to the corporation of a visit programme, to set out a desirable routine and to make provision for the unusual, to suggest additions, and to curtail excessive expenditure.

The specialists

Specialist visitors include the auditors, tax experts and production executives. Each of these functions has its own structure, with procedures, standards and controls, all codified in the departmental manuals. Apart from dealing with current issues, expert visitors also have 'control' roles.

The financial auditors are a normal feature of organizational life, often welcomed for their advice and help. Nevertheless, there are invariably questions on procedures, financial lapses and irregularities. Communication management requires that formal findings are first reviewed with the local office to get matters put right. Future cooperation can be jeopardized should findings only filter back by way of head office admonition and criticism.

Auditors can be used in a wider role, to compare procedures and systems between markets. For instance, the cost of meetings, events and travel is seldom analysed and, if done, is only of value when compared on a like basis between markets. Given the same definitions, an office can appear to spend inordinately on sales meetings – but should that unit be particularly successful, then other markets might be wise to increase spend in this area. Unfortunately, the alternative is more likely to be true, the frequent-meeting, high-profile spending organization showing below-average results.

Travel and entertainment can be a sensitive area but again, comparing like with like across markets can be illuminating – and lead to useful saving. In general, the auditing function is under-used, given little encouragement to exercise analytical skill outside the financial area. The marginal cost of wider involvement is negligible but the saving can be significant.

The visiting production executive has an important routine in checking the correct application of safety procedures. Regular, fastidious inspection is not always the rule and, in the pressure of events, overlooked and forgotten. It does not need a factory to blow up for a company to face disaster from an accident.

In the managed communication environment, such procedures are set out in the policy manuals and the visit programme is monitored to ensure that the necessary reports have been filed. These are reviewed at head office for matters of common interest to be advised through the network.

Maximizing the use of reports

Much of communication in a world corporation has to be in writing and, where possible, in standard format for ready consolidation and use. Essential reports includes those on materials, output and stocks; sales, cash and the profit-and-loss balance sheet and budget returns.

Over and above the basic requirements, a world group has the in-house ability to acquire much of the intelligence necessary for the management of change. Each operating entity is in touch with the local environment and, given company-wide management of communication, is expected to keep the network updated on its market.

Instant connections can encourage the immediate, excited reporting of local events, before time brings some perspective to a situation. Such ad hoc reporting should decline with maturity. The international houses have seen currency changes and trade restrictions before and managers are expected to come up with appraisal, possible courses of action, and not simply report the news. In any event, that will have appeared in the press.

Standard formats and laid-down procedures help to keep matters in focus.

However, no amount of reports or formal structuring of meetings and visiting will guarantee that a corporation will stay ahead and not discover too late that the world has changed and it no longer has a place. It has happened throughout history and is happening today, whether to mainframe computers, sugar cane or the armaments complex.

Large organizations create business intelligence units to study trends and forecast market change. Their output is helpful in guiding investment decisions, the allocation of resources between markets and product groups but much of the work can be based on 'old' statistics and information. In the time it takes to collect and process data into intelligence, then to study individual investments and reach decisions, the situation may have altered drastically. It has happened twice with real estate and property, worldwide, in less than 20 years, each time with large investment groups going ahead with projects despite the collapse and then facing bankruptcy before completion.

To stay the pace, the internationals have a flexible communication network. Perhaps the best-served industry is that of pharmaceuticals. The manufacturers of drugs and medicines have direct access via terminals on the desks of individual executives to commercial databases which bring them the pattern of sales and consumption around the globe. The data are backed by sophisticated analysis and projection formulae and tailored to in-house requirements.

It is no coincidence that an industry which has supported a communication network at the forefront of technology and global in scope has been rewarded with unrivalled prosperity since the Second World War.

Similar information is available to food manufacturers. Other sectors sponsor the collection of market data but much information has still to be sourced from governments or obtained through voluntary data exchange schemes. Such material tends to be dated and is not always subjected to the scrutiny applied to commercial services. It has the complication of varying definitions and formats and content is geared to the requirements of the sponsoring department and not the commercial user.

Culture and environment

Business statistics apart, a managed communications network will carry a cultural and environmental fact file on each market. This will hold such practical information as the legislative and regulatory framework, e.g. the labelling and packaging requirements, advertising restrictions. It will also carry such details of the market structure as the distribution system, the industry set-up and employment practices.

All this saves much individual effort in the searching for data and also forewarns of potential difficulties in the way of proposals, e.g. whether a new formula will be approved or an advertisement permitted.

More subtle is to record the corporate experience of each market. Colour, for example, is of significance in many countries and has to be kept in mind for packaging and advertising. A comprehensive database carries details of customs, habits and behaviour, the background information invaluable to visitors and new employees.

SUMMARY

The principles of international communication are those that apply to any market.

To work globally, the individual must assume responsibility for understanding habits and customs and the behaviour expected in different countries. Where English is used, it is done with an understanding of local sensitivities.

Stereotyping is seen as dangerous and to be avoided.

The multinational corporation has the advantage of diversity of experience and of the varying approaches to different markets and among its employees. All this is recognized as resource and exploited by a managed network. The systems are put in place to offer guidance on every aspect of operations, from recruitment and training to the routines for personal contact, from the annual cycle of meetings to the planning and budgeting procedures.

10

THE BARRIERS TO COMPANY-WIDE COMMUNICATION

The barriers to effective company-wide communication are identified. These hurdles are discussed in terms of organization, personality, inertia and complacency.

INTRODUCTION

The achievement of effective communication calls for continuing effort.

Why? What are the difficulties?

The barriers to communication are made up of four elements:

- **complacency**, arising out of the belief that all is and remains well;
- an **unwillingness** to face and handle change;
- an outdated organizational **structure**;
- individual attitudes and the **secrecy** syndrome.

These hurdles are never completely cleared and require the continuing attention of communication management.

It is unfortunate that communication cannot be seen or measured in terms of direct monetary value, as producing a result in plus or minus terms against the budget for the year. It is the great intangible, the system that can remain unnoticed until the show comes to an end. Then, when it is too late for anything to be done, communication is recognized for what it is, the nerve structure that was the key to successful activity and has been allowed to fail.

The situation is illustrated by the remarks of a noted post-war inno-vator, successful in Britain, in Europe and the USA who, on being ousted from his empire, admitted:

> I have made mistakes. I've never managed to get around me people who were able to run the administrative side of the busi-ness as efficiently as it should have been run. That's not my talent. I know it has to be done and the criticism could be made that I've picked poor people (Sir Terence Conran, founder of Habitat).

Here is a man whose instinctive communication with the market kept him at the forefront of change, to the extent of creating trends, but who did not recognize in time that the function is all-embracing. The ability to listen to the market, so outstanding a talent in this case, was not matched by attention to the internal structure, to maintaining company-wide communication.

COMPLACENCY IN THE FACE OF CHANGE

The life-cycle of an enterprise starts with the entrepreneur recognizing or being in a position to exploit a moment of change, with a product, a system, an organizational innovation. One way it ends is as a monolith, as did the old Rolls Royce, talking internally and chattering away into oblivion.

Study of long-term, continuing market leadership and success – a Shell company, Unilever or a DuPont – highlights the regularity of renewal that stems from change at the top. The term of senior posi-tions is limited and each new team realigns the business to the market and also looks at the internal structure. It may not be recognized as such by those involved, but much of these exercises is a refocusing of links and structures, in effect updating communication.

Each of these great enterprises has not only survived but grown during times of adversity and upheaval. Shell, for instance, had a few short years in the 1950s in which to adjust from a privileged, almost imperial role to the full market force environment. The corporation's success, first in recognizing the need and then in making the transition was founded in market awareness – and its ability to meet the new situation with radical internal change.

Re-engineering

Success carries with it the danger of complacency, a belief that the market continues to be understood even while it continues to change. Help in maintaining market contact can come from employing outside skills – the advertising agency, market research or the public relations consultancy introduce fresh thinking and insight to change. In parallel the internal network cannot be left to chance, to a dated structure and uncoordinated individual initiative that is not in a position to face the overall imperatives.

A current mode for change is to 're-engineer', to replace the traditional structure of running functions such as sales and production by departments with teams responsible for and delivering the core operations. A leading exponent of this approach, James Champy, chairman of the CSG Index consultancy, notes that difficulties arise because managers 'do not really have an appetite for discontinuous and radical change – and all the pain that goes with it'.

Meeting change, he points out, is not only a matter of updating processes but also involves altering management structures and behaviour. He believes that in the modern environment the life-cycles of businesses that do not position themselves for change are shortening.

Why change if matters are going well? Champy is convinced only a small proportion of corporations that believe they are restructuring are in fact doing so. Instead a given operation is reorganized, or a product line rebuilt but there is no noticeable improvement for the corporation as a whole.

One of the quoted problems of re-engineering centres on the difficulty of defining the core model around which the structure is to be built, the market links developed. It is a problem indicative of, and arising from, tenuous communication, a failure to manage the function. Managers might well have no 'appetite' for change if their view of the market is obscure, if there is no urgent appreciation of the potentials and threats of current change.

THE ORGANIZATIONAL BARRIERS

Analysis of core functions, and the structures required to support them, can be a difficult task in organizations that have operations functioning in relative isolation, without the close links of a developed network. The objective of each unit has been to make the current budget, with little knowledge of and only cursory interest in what is happening elsewhere.

There is no team, only players shooting individually at goal and in doing so remaining unaware when the posts are moved. Unchallenging routine creates the inertia that builds barriers. The process may be unconscious but the barriers are real nevertheless.

Finance

Inadequate, dated financial information, whether at management or operational level, is an obvious shortcoming. It is relatively easy to put right but, without systematic review, an unsound system will continue to run, until there is a disaster. Poor financial data on current affairs or true costs, is almost invariably quoted as a cause when corporations fail.

At the same time, competent audited accounts are no guarantee of the existence of actionable information for management. It is ironic that this proved to be the case at the leading communication shop, Saatchi & Saatchi, when a global turndown of business revealed not only the precariousness of the financial structure but also the inadequacy of the data available for dealing with the situation.

A new management and a much-strengthened accounting function allowed the business to survive but only at considerable cost to the shareholders and employees. Once again, an outstandingly successful business had failed to ensure the adequacy of communication, which in this case was its own area of expertise. The original management had 'failed to listen' by not ensuring that the intelligence essential to their task was to hand, that the facts were supportive of their actions and decisions.

The budget

Poor communication of the budget, restricting knowledge of the objectives, leaves employees working with no aim beyond that of the daily task. There may be some incentives to improve output or the services but people are given no vision and do not feel involved. They are not called upon to communicate and remain passive, whatever their theoretical links to the network.

The market

There is danger in accepting at face value the claims of operational management to have a full understanding of the marketplace, the 'our staff are long-serving and know their business' assumption. Activity is allowed to continue without the discipline of detailed assessment of what is happening in the market, with no admission that much may be happening that is not known.

Such data as are captured by the reporting system, or brought in by the agencies and consultants, are used tactically, day-by-day, but not distributed or coordinated for corporate or overall planning. There is no recognized communication network or sense of moving the whole organization forward, in jointly identifying and meeting change.

The operational structure

In a faulty organization, the operating units and specialist functions have no common meeting ground and no recognized lines of contact. The links to and between production and distribution, design and R & D and specialist functions and product management are weak.

There is particular value in having outside consultants review operations or specific aspects when a business is static or beginning to face unusual difficulties and is no longer progressing. Outside experts have the advantage of experience across industry in similar and disparate organizations and are unfettered by historic precedent and practice.

Whatever the brief, much of consultants' work lies in the study of communication, in examining the adequacy of data, the flow of intelligence and the linkage of each operation into the network. A common assignment is to review **pricing policy**. Such a study begins with the consultant examining the market structure to establish existing ways of doing business, the approaches adopted by other players, what it is that best meets needs or indeed remains valid.

The consultant will go on to pose alternatives: package instead of individual pricing (spares, pharmaceutical supply contracts) or fees to replace commissions (advertising and insurance). Whatever the validity of the various approaches, it is the in-house reactions to them that are revealing. Should these remain rigid, with only half-hearted willingness to discuss the possibilities, then management has probably allowed links with the market to weaken or has lost the capacity to absorb and understand the dynamics of change. The time has come for a more fundamental examination of this corporation and its structure.

Production is another area in which consultants are commonly employed. Again, the study will reveal the extent to which management is aware of changing technology and new approaches.

Examination of the **distribution system** tests elements of both internal and external communication. A study reveals the level of in-house understanding of the full costs and the restraints of distribution. Also established is what management knows of possible alternatives and the new approaches being developed outside, of the strength of external communication links.

New thinking and people management

The sclerotic organization has no room for the maverick, no channel for the outrageous idea or comment. Much that is outlandish may be irritating but it only takes one original idea, one 'tiger in the tank', to bring new life into the entire enterprise.

Management is not an entirely rational process, emotion plays a role in leading people and inspiring effort. Business follows other walks of life in taking to fashion, most obviously by embracing important-sounding concepts. There is always a vogue, running over the years from the time-and-motion studies that at one time caused so much anguish to such current concepts as 'downsizing' (perhaps to claim a place on the 'information highway'!).

The alert, the Falcons, anxious to take their place out front, communicate in the new jargon and this may all lead to improvement and keeping pace with change. More importantly, there is flexibility and a willingness to look at the new and the different. There is an element of excitement, of intellectual questioning.

A workforce expects more than to be given information only sufficient to the daily task, how to switch on the machine and schedule the day. People want and expect to be involved and respond accordingly.

More onerous legal requirements result in even small enterprises having a personnel function. This office may confine itself to the statutory, to staff programmes and entitlements or it may look a little wider and, for instance, produce the in-house publications.

That is satisfactory as far as it goes but internal communication cannot be left to the personnel manager and his or her perception of what is required. In the company-wide communication environment, with every employee linked to the network, the personnel office is a valuable element but it cannot be the only, or even the main, link with the workforce at large. A managed communication network integrates all activity with operations as a whole.

PERSONALITY AND THE SECRECY SYNDROME

An opaque but very real barrier to building the communication network is the secrecy syndrome. This can be part of the management ethos but is also a strong trait in many personalities. There are limits to what can be communicated but necessary discretion does not equate with secrecy.

Publication of a detailed marketing plan or of price structures is clearly not desirable in a competitive situation. Market arrangements may well be jeopardized by disclosures and there are legal limits to what directors can discuss and say about the business.

In the final analysis, however, nothing is confidential. Even the greatest of state secrets come to light, seemingly sooner rather than later nowadays, but ordinary life continues. There is no breakdown of society because a president or minister is shown to have human feet of clay or there has been questionable business activity. Even a scandal of unbelievable magnitude, the corruption saga of Italy, has not caused chaos.

Nevertheless, for many it is natural to maintain what is seen as discretion. Others find that possession of information equates with power, or at least gives a satisfying illusion of power, a sense of importance and of privilege. These people usually need to have others aware of their 'insider' status and are great originators of rumour. A hint at coming events and projected developments, while maintaining the aura of tight-lipped confidentiality on specifics, feeds the personal ego but opens cracks in the organization.

The result is an atmosphere of unease and uncertainty, and lowered morale. Speculation and gossip are a poor use of time and energy. Further damage is caused by disbelief of the official 'line', when and if there is one, and an unfortunate air of general mistrust is generated.

Secrecy is also expensive to arrange and maintain physically, directly in terms of extra equipment, the private telex perhaps, and more importantly, in staff arrangements. It is almost a truism that the 'confidential' tag on any item attracts attention; the same information in an unmarked document or message is ignored.

Meltdown

The subject is one of wider significance. In an increasingly complex world, where there are dangers and pitfalls inherent in so much of activity, damage can be done that is sometimes not obvious for years, even decades ahead. The processes for the open discussion of plans and developments can be painful and even abused by vested interests. On the other hand, inviting detailed scrutiny, both internally and also as widely as possible by outside interests, does mean that every aspect is examined, at least as well as current knowledge allows. If nothing else, the moral duty has been done.

Any system that hides faults until there is a nuclear meltdown is in terminal mode.

Assessing the need for secrecy

A corporation can make a rational assessment of the usually very limited material that needs to be kept confidential for the good of the enterprise (as opposed to the satisfaction of individual egos). Starting from the premise that with hindsight nothing is confidential, the areas genuinely requiring caution can be identified. These usually relate to current commercial policies and to aspects of research; all else is 'open', if not actively published.

In the best-known situation, that of asbestos, the claims have been running for decades and on such a scale as to create serious difficulties not only for the manufacturers and others immediately involved, but also for the insurance markets. The extent of the problem has been magnified by original failures to communicate, to make known and have discussed the dangers to health as soon as the first evidence appeared. The lesson has not been absorbed: major subsequent class actions for damages have almost invariably alleged the cover-up of data, the failure to communicate as reason for exemplary damages.

Once the principle has been recognized and accepted, it is not an area of great difficulty for the communication portfolio holder to keep under review.

Unusual accountancy practices, product problems, factory disasters or skew marketing tactics create havoc when 'revealed' as opposed to being announced and explained. The instinctive reaction to mistakes, themselves perhaps only obvious with hindsight, is the defensive, to deny or obscure.

Often management can be seen to have been lax with controls or to have shown poor judgment, in effect, to have failed to manage. Denial or salami-slice disclosure is then a recipe for disaster. The outstanding examples of such failure include the 1980s junk bond and then the Savings & Loan disasters in the US. These situations were perhaps creatures of their time but none the less resulted in the loss of billions and the guillotine for many careers.

Much of the damage would have been mitigated, if not avoided, had managements and regulators done the job they were paid to do and insisted on methods and procedures being explained and discussed, in fact, if they had communicated. Instead, seemingly successful individuals were allowed to operate unmonitored, unquestioned and called to no account until events overwhelmed them, their colleagues and customers.

In the company-wide communication environment, every senior executive is expected to contribute to the security review, to specify the confidential in relevant areas of responsibility. In the final analysis it is for the board of directors or executive committee to ensure that any such barriers are watched and kept to an irreducible minimum, that there is an understood way of doing things, a corporate ethos. The communication portfolio is given guidance and a policy on which to work.

One chairman of a leading multinational clearly understands the situation when he points in his annual report to his aims for improving the complex of relationships between departments, between his various companies and their suppliers and customers.

> During times of change – and we are living in one now – innovation is especially important. Of course there has always been change. But now, unlike the past, change is regarded by many people not as a challenge, as an opportunity for renewal and the conquest of new shores, but as a threat.

> The times are marked by uncertainty as to where we are headed. Various circumstances contribute to this state of affairs: for example, the unfathomable proliferation of knowledge and the associated information explosion, and the interaction of national and international events and processes.

> All aspects of life are affected by them – religion, politics are and, last but not least, the economy ... [all] this aims at improving the complex relationships between different departments and between ourselves and our suppliers and customers, by discussing and clarifying the requirements of both parties and

then meeting them one hundred percent. Sources of error are identified and lastingly corrected (Dr Alex Krauer, Ciba-Geigy, Basle).

The pace of change, the 'unfathomable' complexities in which the enterprise operates, makes communication a prime concern of this continuing, successful management.

SUMMARY

Company-wide communication can be frustrated by organizational barriers and by individual attitudes.

Many of these hurdles can be readily identified and removed. Sometimes outside expertise is helpful in ensuring the adequacy of management information and of the control procedures.

The penchant for secrecy by some individuals has to be recognized. The scope of necessary discretion can be defined and is then kept under review by the communication portfolio holder.

11

MONITORING COMPANY-WIDE COMMUNICATION

The Communication Health Index is based on an annual 'audit ' of the effectiveness of the network. Primary concerns are to ensure that the organization is attuned to continued change in the marketplace and that the staff both are and feel themselves to be involved. The adequacy of the reporting structure, the functioning of the central desk and cost/benefit analysis of the meetings cycle are other elements of the Index.

INTRODUCTION

The functioning of company-wide communication is 'audited' to ensure that the network is:

- an effective monitor of the market and of change; and
- fully operational internally.

The audit is carried out annually as part of the planning and budget cycle, under the supervision of the director holding the portfolio, and is assessed overall in the form of the Communication Health Index. The audit is an established routine, not one relegated into a periodic or piecemeal exercise.

AWARENESS OF MARKET CHANGE

There is no secret to change: the new is published, presented in public, broadcast. The audit checks that these data are being captured systematically, where necessary by the use of market research and customer polling, and that it is understood and absorbed. The corporation must be capable of assessing the potential impact of change on current operations and methods, for opening opportunities and for revealing threats.

The task of assessing the capability for turning data into actionable intelligence is necessarily subjective but lies at the heart of management. It can be critical to have a senior director step back and look at operations in this way. Two examples, widely different in time and place, illustrate the point.

The failure to change

The Swiss watch industry viewed the advent of electronic technology in the 1960s with complacency. The traditional manufacturers, who had for so long dominated the world market, could not accept or absorb the potential impact either of the new methods for accurate, low-cost time-keeping but also did not realize that the market itself was changing. The conservative buyer was being overtaken by youthful fashion.

The loss of market share was ignored until reflected in actual sales declines, first to the youth market and then in the boutiques of the fashion-conscious trendsetters. Rebuilding their business took the Swiss over a decade, a long, expensive and painful process. It has also proved to be an outstandingly successful programme but there is now no industry that monitors the markets of the world more closely than do the watchmakers of Switzerland.

Thirty years later and the situation is particularly dramatic in the computer industry. Wang, one of the outstanding success stories of the 1970s and '80s, was bankrupt a decade later. One commentator summarized the position: Wang 'failed to realize the importance of the advent of the personal computer ... how fast it would make certain other systems obsolete'. Advancing, even galloping change, had made the older, more expensive computer systems obsolete, leaving Wang stranded.

The dominance achieved by Japanese enterprise in traditional manufactured goods, ranging from motorcycles to ship-building, is further and eloquent testimony to the damage flowing from communication failure. The long-established industrialists of both Europe and the USA failed to acknowledge and then to absorb information on new technology and changing methods that was freely communicated and known to all.

Japanese competition took a generation to develop, working all along with known plans and programmes. At the time, the resources and capacities of the Western manufacturers far exceeded those available to the newcomers but they ignored the data or failed to absorb the implications and to realize the significance of what was happening.

It can be argued that the manufacturers of the West had to contend with an entirely different social and economic structure. True, but hard to accept. Given the will and ability to absorb data and turn it into intelligence, the realization that oblivion threatened would have been a powerful incentive to change outdated habits and structures. In fact, it had been done just a little earlier by the same manufacturers, when methods, such as those employed in shipbuilding, were revolutionized in order to win a war.

The fact was that, after years of booming business, of working to capacity, manufacturers, ranging from those of bicycles to ocean shipping, had become unable to listen, had closed their minds to developments in the market.

The Japanese, on the other hand, have so far stayed with the game, learned to handle continuing change as they in turn face competition. Every Japanese manufacturer has a running programme of improvement and innovation and, where necessary, of structural change. One example is the willingness to move manufacturing capacity overseas, e.g. the car factories set up in the UK in order to overcome the restrictions of the European market.

AUDITING COMMUNICATION EFFECTIVENESS

Assessing the effectiveness of the network to monitor change can be done by using a few simple instruments and techniques. Extra costs are not involved, only a willingness to use both the existing structures and the intelligence that is produced through them. The capacity to assess change must also exist.

The commentary change list

One start point is to have each departmental head note the significant changes seen in the previous 12-month period. This is a simple listing, usually forming part of the introductory commentary accompanying the annual plan.

There is no need for this change list to be a complex report, with detailed explanations against each point. After all, each item on such a list should be known, in terms of background and impact, by colleagues making up the working team and the relevant staff. When reviewed or circulated, change lists reveal gaps in what is known or needed to have been known but not communicated during the year. Extra links can then be forged for the more efficient operation of the whole group.

Change lists have other uses. They can be input to strategic, long-range planning, helping to answer the 'where do we stand now?' question that is part of the process. They are also valuable in handover notes during a change of management. More subtly, a list helps judge the competence of managers, testing their knowledge of the market and their ability to distinguish the important fundamentals that make the difference.

People developments

The change list covers the people events of the year. Internal movements include important promotions, the acquisition by employees of special skills and qualifications, their election to trade bodies and perhaps also significant achievements outside the business.

Similarly, important changes in the customer and client base are noted, as are moves in management and of buyers and opinion leaders. This 'news' can be checked against the customer databases to ensure these were updated as events occurred during the year. It is also possible to question whether contact in the market is directed to the best advantage, focused on the right people and that the corporation itself is well integrated with the industry organizations and representative bodies.

Price movements

The change list records important movements in prices over the period of raw materials and other costs on the one hand, of product and market price levels or of fees on the other. Apart from any value as a ready historic reference, these data help other product groups or offices and the staff functions to understand the dynamics of the business. Price movements are a pointer to the pressures faced and the actions taken during the period.

Products and markets

Also prominent on the change lists are product or service upgrades and developments. Launches, new techniques and enhancements, own and competitive, are noted, together with any innovative marketing approaches or activity.

Change often results from developments outside the direct market-place. The notable example of recent years is the criss-cross complex of developments in the handling of data and information. At any given time, a software company manager might list half-a-dozen directly competitive services, note hardware enhancements that will impact his or her range of packages, and then also record a fundamental change, perhaps a new input system or direct linkages that have the potential to alter his or her entire way of doing business.

In recognition of the outlook, the plans for the year will take into account the factors of immediate impact but, being aware, the alert manager will also keep a watchful eye on the potential threat posed by the changing fundamentals. Sometimes developments have been brought to light by market research or customer polling and it is help-ful for a change list to note the studies carried out during the year. Market studies are expensive investments and, when recorded in this way, it is possible to check that the mechanism exists and has been used during the year for the data to have been made known and avail-able to other units and interested colleagues.

The central desk

Given the key role of the central desk to networking, the in-house publications and in the update of the databases, assessment of its effi-ciency is part of the audit process. The first objective is to ensure that management's communication requirements coincide with how the desk views its functions. The framework will be set out in the policy manual but much of the effectiveness of such a post will depend on the individual.

Basis for the function is the input of material to the desk: are all reports originating above a given organizational level being copied to the chief executive? Are reporting requirements being met and, if not, how are matters to be put right? Is the desk kept aware of all market research and polling?

The central desk itself has a monitor role, to check that reporting is timely, in correct format and adequate in content. Integrity of the data is important. For example, familiar competition is dropped and no longer mentioned in reports, although continuing to make an impact with activities that could be duplicated elsewhere. The market involved is asked for an update and reminded that what might be routine locally is not necessarily the case elsewhere.

A technological change might only be noticed by one office – what is happening in other markets? The follow-up programme of an alert central desk will have such gaps filled.

The central desk can also have a coordination responsibility for company-wide expenditure in two important areas: subscriptions to the ever-expanding networks of commercial databases and the employment of consultants. The audit checks that the lists are complete and are being used to eliminate duplication and to ensure the best use of these resources.

Some of the shortcomings revealed by staff polling may point to the Central Desk but in general, review of its functions is on a personal level. The director holding the communication portfolio sits down, perhaps with one or two colleagues, and discusses the operation with the executive(s) concerned.

The reporting structure

The central desk apart, each operation is also asked during the audit process to comment on the adequacy of the information received and on the perceived value of what it is required to transmit.

The simple enquiry of a manager, 'Are you receiving all the information you need, is it clear and on time?', opens a wide-ranging discussion. This review can take place at the person-to-person level, be carried out by questionnaire or form part of the planning cycle.

Clarity of the data is a function of common definitions. It needs to be clear, for instance, that the sales figure represents actual shipments, less returns, and includes goods supplied to group companies. There are other variations and a 'clarity' exercise, having those involved actually quote the definitions, can reveal surprising misunderstandings and long-established routines that are wrong.

Graphs can easily mislead and the advantage of having an established standard form of illustration may outweigh the impact of inhibiting creative freedom, at least for the routine internal analyses.

Conciseness: over-written material is expensive, both at the point of production and for the recipient office to use. It is a matter for individual contact but a house style can be useful. Perhaps all reports are required to carry a half-page summary, no routine memorandum is to exceed a page, with points of detail and supporting arguments noted in appendices. Minutes of meetings might normally be restricted to recording conclusions.

Such provision may seem bureaucractic but a streamlined system can enhance understanding and improve efficiency. It is worth effort to achieve a routine the results of which are seen to be compatible with the effort devoted to input. The audit should not reveal resentment at the flow of paper or that routine reporting is felt to be excessive.

The **completeness** and **timeliness** of reporting is judged against the established requirements, normally to be found in the policy manual. However, does operational management feel in possession of all information relevant to the budget programme? Is each unit aware of what is happening elsewhere, with products and competitors, marketing and technology?

These facts should be available through the routine of planning meetings and on the databases. Any gaps revealed by the audit are, in the previously quoted words of Dr Kraurer, to be 'lastingly corrected ... one hundred percent'.

Other advantages of an annual audit of communication include the review first of the internal databases, with a view to the removal of accumulated garbage, and also the links with world databases. Are all the subscription services still of continuing relevance? At the same time, the potential value of new sources of data coming on-stream can be evaluated systematically.

Systems are subjected to continuing development, the introduction of new files and the creation of additional linkages. The tinkering and amendment of systems is wearisome and often confusing to the user. An annual well-documented update is one welcomed outcome of the audit programme.

Meetings

One major activity that is not controlled by management is that of meetings. Events are known to take place but there is no data on how often or why people are spending time in meetings. Occasionally there is concern, and a suspicion that there is waste in this uncontrolled use of valuable resource, and sporadic attempts are made to limit meetings by arbitrary decisions. (These may result in yet more meetings to discuss the issue!)

The aim is to get people to spend time on their work, not in talking about it but the questions remain. How much time is being spent in meetings? Which gatherings are considered useful? Where can matters be improved and what occasions are felt to be wastes of time? What results are being achieved?

Meetings are of great diversity and individuality, the likely explanation for the area being ignored as a management opportunity, and finding answers is not easy. The annual audit strives for an assessment which, in a corporation of any size, is developed from a sample. This can be based on all the meetings held during a given week or fortnight or on those held over a period at locations that are broadly representative of the organization. A sample can also be picked to reflect each function, e.g. a month's meetings at one or two sales offices, in a production unit or by representative marketing groups.

A meeting can perhaps be defined as an event for which notice has been given at least a day in advance. The basic structural meetings, such as those of the board, the executive committee and the formal budget sessions, should these coincide with the sample period, are excluded from the process. All attending a meeting that is part of the sample complete a simple return which confirms both the purpose and how long the occasion lasted and gives ratings for such criteria as:

- efficiency of organization;
- relevance to the topic;
- relevance to the respondent;
- actionability of the results;
- value against equivalent time on the job.

There is space for subjective comment and the returns are handled in confidence, perhaps at the central desk or by the auditors. A rating is developed which at its simplest would look something like that shown in Table 11.1.

The five criteria might not be considered to have equal importance and the next step would be to introduce a weighting factor (Table 11.2).

Such analyses are helpful to a manager seeking to improve the quality of meetings being held in the unit or operation. Any criterion can be measured and action taken to improve that aspect or to up-grade a given set or type of meeting. If the 'relevance to me' rating is consistently low, perhaps too many people are being invited to attend events; where a meeting continues to have a high score, the convenor might be able to help colleagues who are running poorly regarded events. When repeated over time, the ratings help to chart hopefully positive development.

Table 11.1 Simple rating of meeting

	Very good:2	Good: 1	Average: 0	Poor: -1	Very poor: -2	Total marks
Organization	(1) 2	(2) 2	(3) -	- -	- -	4
Relevance to topic	- -	(5) 5	(1) -	- -	- -	5
Relevance to me	- -	(1) 1	(5) -	- -	- -	1
Actionability	(1) 2	(2) 2	(2) -	(1) -1	- -	4
Use of time		(3) 3	(2) -	(1) -1	- -	2

Total score		16
Total possible (2 marks × 5 topics × 6 attendances)		60
Index (16 × 100 ÷ 60)		26.6

Notes
Meeting attendance: 6; votes are in parentheses.

Table 11.2 Meeting rating with weighting factor

	Weight factor	Very good:2	Good: 1	Average: 0	Poor: -1	Very poor: -2	Total marks
Organization	0.5	(1) 2	(2) 2	(3) -	- -	- -	2.0
Relevance to topic	2.5	- -	(5) 5	(1) -	- -	- -	12.5
Relevance to me	2.0	- -	(1) 1	(5) -	- -	- -	2.0
Actionability	3.0	(1) 2	(2) 2	(2) -	(1) -1	- -	9.0
Use of time	2.0		(3) 3	(2) -	(1) -1	- -	4.0

Total score		29.5
Total possible (60 marks × weights)		120.0
Index (29.5 × 100 ÷ 120)		24.6

Notes
Meeting attendance: 6; votes are in parentheses.

Other factors arise in attempting to assess and compare meetings, notably in relating the 'value' of the topic to the 'cost of the input', the cost of the event. One basis that helps comparison is that of the time taken by a meeting, that is multiplying the number of particpants by the length of the event. The meeting rated in Tables 11.1 and 11.2 may have lasted three hours which, with six participants, gives an attendance of l8 hours. The record of four meetings may be as shown in Table 11.3.

Table 11.3 Rating of meeting times

		Index	÷	*Hours*	*Net score*
Meeting	1	26.6		18	1.5
	2	35.0		16	2.2
	3	80.0		24	3.3
	4	85.0		60	1.4

In these terms, the meeting with the highest index comes out with the lowest net score. Perhaps an attempt can be made to modify the figures further by assigning a topic 'value' to each event and a factor for the level of participation (i.e. the seniority of those attending, a measure of the cost).

All the ratings for meetings in each cell of the sample can be combined to give a figure for the unit and this can in turn be compared with the results achieved by similar offices. Finally, a meetings' rating is developed for the whole company, as a measure of effectiveness for the area and as an element of the Communication Health Index.

The act of undertaking the exercise and of circulating and explaining the results, heightens awareness of what meetings involve in terms of time and expense. Cost/benefit thinking is encouraged. Without being too rigid, there is a review of the guidelines for meetings, of the procedures and authority for holding them, of making a measurable improvement to the productivity of a major item of the company's costs

The internal review

The continuing effort to keep everyone fully involved with and linked into the network is underlined by the audit. There are the two aspects to check:

- Communication with the employees. This is at two levels. The first is concerned with the adequacy of information on personnel affairs and staff benefits. The other is a check of employee perception of involvement in the company's overall affairs and decisions, of being kept in touch with progress and development.
- The effectiveness of the individual contributions and how closely people feel themselves to be linked to the network.

The staff poll

A standard communication audit technique is the staff poll or questionnaire (see end-of-chapter pro-forma), ideally undertaken by independent professionals. They can be the in-house market researchers but, periodically at least, outside consultants run the programme. The latter have the advantage of being seen as neutral and are more able to supplement written responses with direct interviews. The polls are rated and indexed (as illustrated for meetings) but, as no assumptions have to be made, the results are firmer. The attitudes of one sales force can be compared to that of another, the degree of satisfaction among staff in an operating unit can be charted from year to year.

It is normal for people to want more information and to believe that the full story has still to be told, and, in consequence, it can be difficult to get a high rating for the state of internal communication. Nevertheless, periodic polling, or a rolling programme through departments or divisions, does give management an indication of the perceived adequacy of current arrangements and of the value of the consultation group, the publications and the electronic messaging. Hopefully, as difficulties are recognized and overcome, an upward trend in the overall ratings is achieved.

Communication expectations are not likely to be met '100%', any more than other elements of the operational mix, but it is important to establish that essential information, objectives and targets, are understood and seen to be fully communicated. When people feel that they are informed of and linked to the plans and programmes, and have a live connection with the personnel function, communication is likely to be perceived as adequate, perhaps even satisfactory.

The structure of staff polls

The areas commonly worth studying through the staff poll include the following.

Training Does the workforce see itself as well-trained and highly motivated? Do individuals feel their skills to be recognized and fully used? At the other end of the spectrum, people should not see themselves as being unduly stressed.

Skilled professional polling can be very revealing. Earning a living and putting food on the table is the main motivation for working but 'social' factors have a significant influence on how well it is done, the degree of commitment. Research always shows that while people like to work they also want to feel good about what they are doing, to be involved. An aspect of satisfaction for many comes from having the opportunity to stay abreast of new skills, to upgrade qualifications and meet the challenge of change at the personal level.

Physical environment Physical facilities can have a significant effect on the atmosphere of the workplace. The staff's perception of the light and air, of heating levels, cleanliness and the state of the decor are all worthy of study. A minor improvement, perhaps the provision of paper tissues in the ladies' room, can have a disproportionate affect on morale. Industrial designers and architects do not necessarily have the right answer to every situation and there is usually room for improvement when facilities are viewed from the standpoint of the daily user.

Perception of care and benefit Is the compensation package being communicated? The most expensive element is probably the pension scheme and it is likely to be the least understood. Many UK executives have a major and continuing concern about their car entitlement, even when much of this benefit is taxed. For others, time off and holiday entitlement is the immediate interest.

The fact is that perception of benefits varies and also alters over time. Pension provision has rightly become a major concern and every scheme has its intricacies for the individual. Periodically each benefit is open to review and such questions arise as to whether everyone should be required to take a minimum-length holiday break and then have a choice with the rest of the entitlement. It is a human trait for minor points to attract attention out of all proportion to their significance, all the more reason for consultation to be seen as satisfactory.

Benefits are designed to gain commitment and dedication. By checking that there is full understanding of what is available, the management of communication sets out to ensure that this is indeed the case.

Involvement Key ingredient of job satisfaction is a sense of involvement, of having some say, if not in the decision-making process, then in aspects of one's own position. Even an apparently minor programme can raise the level of interest and staff participation. There is a competition to improve response time and a prize is offered for the unit answering every telephone call by the third ring. Conditions will vary and there will need to be consultation on the mechanics, that is, full involvement from the start. Later there will be questioning of the longer-term result and whether this programme needs to be repeated or if something else should be done at intervals to keep efficiency at the new higher level.

More sophisticated and sensitive is the use of professional polling to question the organizational structure and effectiveness of current methods. One salutary exercise is to poll the sales force and establish individual perception of the adequacy of the structure and of such aspects as product training, territory alignment, data on customers, the level of support and incentives. There is also a real nettle: assessing the degree of satisfaction with the management structure itself.

Questioning in this area is the province of the specialist, the industrial psychologist, skilled both in the collection of the data and in assessment and interpretation. The role of managed communication is first, and regularly, to raise such questions and then to have them answered.

The feedback

Integral to successful staff polling is feedback of the results, in an open and factual format, eschewing the temptation to water down criticisms and include defensive explanations. Polls not 'acknowledged' by publication of the outcome are not seen to produce results. Future cooperation might then be restricted and cynicism and disillusionment greet further initiatives.

Polls check views and perceptions and, if handled well, are themselves evidence of the corporate interest in dialogue and staff involvement. The implementation of subsequent changes is announced in terms of the polling exercise, underlining management commitment to the team approach.

DEVELOPING THE COMMUNICATION HEALTH INDEX

The main benefit of the monitor of communication flows from the various 'audits'. As the results are probed, issues and opportunities are revealed across the whole spectrum of activity. Here for this unit, it may be shown that staff magazines need an uplift; there we see a potentially more serious issue, that product development teams feel their contact with market feedback is inadequate.

Enhanced communication flows from fuller use and perhaps realignment of existing resources and from ensuring people participation. The director responsible for communication is fortunate in having no lack of opportunities for making improvements, the more so as these seldom call for investment. Aspects of communication can always be improved, if only to keep the function aligned to and meeting changing needs. The audits allow effort to be focused on the more obvious opportunities as these are revealed each year.

Current change apart, it would also be useful to have an overall assessment of the communication network, of the 'state of our nerves', based on an accepted formula and available at least on an annual basis.

The development of a Communication Health Index requires some arbitrary decisions to take into account individual organizational characteristics. No two corporations are alike, each has its own culture, nuances of emphasis and, at any given time, is at a different stage of development.

Probably the most important decision will be to exclude from the calculations the marketing programme itself. Revenue and the whole communication effort behind sales are measured continually in the financial returns and by professional monitor. These reflect hard facts that are the subject of continuous concern, built into the day-to-day management of the organization.

The Communication Health Index seeks to take one step back and measure the state of the company-wide network, to ensure that communication is sound and providing the base from which the revenues and profits flow.

The Index can be built on the input from four sets of ratings:

- The **market's perception** of the products and services, perhaps of the company image. This is arrived at by direct market research, possibly modified by further in-house assessment of customer comments and complaints and the input from the front-line staff. These data are usually developed routinely when seen to be needed during the course of the annual planning cycle. The change lists are one check that the focus continues to be on the market and that the procedures used for the purpose are adequate.
- The results and ratings of the **internal review** and staff polling.
- The ratings from the questionaire research on the **reporting structure**.
- The ratings from the **meetings' assessments**.

The input will vary widely by organization and professional statistical advice is helpful in working out the details of weighting, both within and between the major elements, and for determining the actual structure for calculation. At its simplest, the final Index number emerges from the four summaries of ratings (Table 11.4).

Table 11.4 The Communication Health Index

	Maximum possible	*Points achieved*
Market awareness	150	105
Internal (staff) review	280	150
Report structure	75	50
Meetings	320	200
	825	505

Index: $(505 \times 100 \div 825) = 61$

CONCLUSION

Given the emergence of an Index figure, based on an accepted and understood formula, management is in a position to monitor 'the state of nerves' from year to year. The great intangible of business and organization is put into a factual framework, within which it can be controlled and developed. Communication is recognized as offering the business continuing opportunity.

SUMMARY

The monitor or audit of the communication network is a regular, at least an annual exercise.

The effectiveness of the network to monitor change is checked by such techniques as the change list, an element of the annual plan or budget for each operation.

The effectiveness of the reporting structure is assessed directly with each operating manager and with the coordinating central desk. There is a conscious attempt to measure the value of meetings by a study of a sample of such events.

Staff polling is used to measure the degree of satisfaction with internal communication.

A formula is developed to produce the Index of Communication Health from the results of the audits.

APPENDIX A: CHANGE LISTS

A change list is kept as concise as possible. Events and developments are noted without carrying explanations or qualifications, it being understood that if communication has been effective, these are not necessary.

Subjects covered can include:

People

Internal

- staff and workforce changes;
- extra qualifications acquired/public appointments/election to industry positions.

External

- client personnel changes/new contacts and relationships;
- industry and trade appointments;
- supplier changes.

Marketing

- significant development of competitive products/services;
- campaigns/themes/offers and below-the-line activity;
- cost and pricing changes;
- agreements, joint ventures, alliances;
- distribution.

Markets

- legislation/regulations/quality standards;
- environmental issue/pressure groups;
- technology;
- market research, client and supplier polling.

APPENDIX B: STAFF POLLING

Staff polling is organization or topic-related. Basic questionnaires are usually designed on a value scale, viz:

excellent........good........adequate........poor........none

Topics for polling include:

Organization

- clarity of job definition/perceived career opportunity;
- level of management support/leadership/accessibility of and to management;
- standard and usefulness of equipment/tools/promotional items;
- availability of information/data for the job;
- knowledge of company/plans and progress.

Personal

- training/career structure;
- personnel communication: employment terms/pension/health/other entitlements;
- incentives/perception of improvement programmes;
- physical working environment.

Office

- adequacy of facilities: canteen/rest room/heating;
- environment: light and air/warmth and freshness/noise.

Products and services

- information on the products and services;
- level of training in usage, effectiveness, servicing;
- availability of market data, on competitive activity, marketing, technological change.

12

ENVIRONMENTAL AND NON-COMMERCIAL COMMUNICATION

The major elements of non-commercial communication are environmental management; the monitor of regulatory change; maintaining a contingency plan for handling disaster; and keeping close contact with the financial community and the shareholders.

INTRODUCTION

Over and above running the market and in-house networks, communication management has responsibility for:

- building **relationships** with **community and special interest** groups;
- the **monitoring** of, and involvement in **regulatory change**;
- preparing and keeping current a plan for coping with **disaster**;
- maintaining sound links with the **financial community and shareholders**.

SPECIAL INTERESTS AND THE ENVIRONMENT

Improving environmental performance is not an optional extra, it is an absolute prerequisite if we are to have a continuing licence from the general public to operate (Sir Denys Henderson, Chairman, ICI).

Concern for the environment covers a wide range of issues but manufacturing industry in particular is liable to be subjected to pressure on several fronts.

Groups dedicated to special or individual issues can be unpleasant, strong enough to impact financial stability and even threaten physical harassment, if not worse. Managed communication seeks a constructive channel for this energy.

Sir Denys, in his review, makes the point clear:

> Their anxieties will not go away, no matter how large our efforts to operate in a more environmentally responsible fashion. But we must continue to communicate our improving performance and participate vigorously in the 'debate'.

He adds that while traditional industries are being forced to change technology because of environmental pressure, the chemical industry for one must point to its role in improving the quality of life, from food and clothing to housing, transport and health.

> As an industry, we spend vast sums on research and development, but much less on taking the temperature of those markets we wish to penetrate.

Virtually all activity has side effects. The humblest sandwich bar or fast-food outlet uses wrapping paper and take-away boxes that customers then litter over the surrounding area, distressing residents and consuming local authority cleansing resources.

The point can be taken to the absurd – as is seen in the arguments of some extremists. Our sandwich bar is then equated with the famous butterfly which, in the scenario of Chaos Theory, alters the world climate with the ripples produced by a beat of its wings.

After all, the bar consumes wrapping that would not be required for food prepared in a household kitchen or restaurant. This material is produced from trees with the use of harsh chemicals. Meanwhile, much of the consumption through the bar is on impulse and not strictly necessary for nourishment.

Arguments do run along these ultra-simplistic lines. The environmental model is of baffling complexity, made more opaque by the moral and religious beliefs and attitudes that impinge in so many areas.

Often, too, the lobbies are armed with the great wisdom of hindsight and are always fortunate in having no responsibility for the human and financial costs of implementing the desirable.

In all this cacophony, the business that is called to account has to recognize that the lobbies are made up of the dedicated and the articulate, people not to be swayed by the simplistic, to be further angered by condescension.

An example of change

The management of Tupperware, the leading manufacturer of plastic food containers, officially committed to eco-management and audit schemes, believes that 'the best way to avoid pollution is not to create it in the first place'.

The managing director in Germany, Dr Hans Adelmann, runs a campaign to reduce packing by having people shop with their own plastic containers. The result shown by survey in Berlin has been a 30% reduction in related forms of waste.

The reverse side of that coin, of course, is reduced business and opportunity for the people employed in the production of packaging. The fact that there are no easy solutions in the environmental field adds to the communication challenge.

The strength of managed communication lies in the ability to face issues squarely, in avoiding the temptation of self-obfuscating. Generally, environmental issues do not become threatening overnight and the professional network, one attuned to listen and be aware of events, will capture concern at an early stage. There is then ample time to prepare and adjust to a threatening storm.

Advantage of opposition

The professional communicator recognizes opposition to be as integral to the free market as is competition. Interests juggle for perceived benefits in the way rival producers struggle for sales and market share. Opposition, however irritating, even destructive, has value in guarding against abuse, in the achievement of higher standards. Despite all their problems, the countries of the West have seen nothing to compare with the horrendous scale of devastation now being revealed in Eastern Europe and Russia.

Central planners presumably did what seemed best at the time but without opposition were unable to grasp the broader picture. The ill-judged scheme to take the waters of the Aral Sea for the irrigation of cotton is alone destroying an area the size of France. Not only is the lake being drained but the cottonfields are turning saline.

The communication task is to be alert to threat and, by early warning, allow change and adjustment to blunt if not deflect a problem. Given that difficulty is usually centred on a single site or confined to an operating mode, advance notice of concern is the key to successful defence.

Avoided problems do not feature in statistics. Equally, the role of successful communication cannot be measured. The price of failure, however, is there for all to see.

Seminal cases

In the two seminal cases, Ralph Nader's *Unsafe At Any Speed* exposé of the US automobile industry and Rachel Carson's *Silent Spring* lament against agricultural chemicals, global industries were caught with nonexistent communication.[1] There had been no listening, never mind systematic monitoring or dialogue with the environment. The industries had no warning – and no plan of action.

The costs at the time were enormous and the world has never been the same since for either group of manufacturers. Agricultural chemicals, in particular, have faced a hostile environment ever since.

Currently, meat and specifically the beef industry in the USA, faces the same predicament. Jeremyn Rifkin's book, *Beyond Beef*, is the culmination of years of ignored concerns, dismissed criticisms and it now launches the ultimate attack.[2] The book discusses alleged abuses but only as a means to an end – the abolition or death of the industry itself.

Belatedly, the ranchers and meat processors have been forced to listen and form a defensive lobby, the Food Facts Coalition, to communicate with the market. It seems unlikely that a dialogue can be built across such a battlefield and the industry is already paying a heavy price for its failure to listen and manage communication: the statistics show a sharp drop in the consumption of beef in the US over the past decade.

Beef lies at the core of American culture and the situation proves yet again that nothing is sacred or immune to change – all must listen to the market and the environment.

Realistic reaction

Once under scrutiny or attack, the communication function has the duty of ensuring that the corporation looks at the situation in an open and realistic manner. The first step is to collect the history and all available facts and then to make a full and objective assessment of what has happened or is happening.

The natural reaction is to be defensive, to rationalize and justify. Worse is to obscure the situation and become intellectually dishonest internally, to refuse to face the facts. It is all very understandable but gives no basis for communicating or for constructive debate.

In many cases there are no clear-cut answers, no simple solutions – otherwise, of course, problems would quickly be overcome, without controversy or sanction. The accuser usually has an in-built advantage, often that of the small voice crying out against powerful interests. The communication aim is to open a discussion, to talk and avoid the sterility of charge and counter-charge.

A situation or proposal is usually subject to varying interpretations and, from the viewpoint of the 'accused', some of the criticism can appear unfair and perhaps malicious. Even in such circumstances, managed communication will seek to keep the debate open, be willing to put forward a balanced argument, one seen to be based on clear and careful analysis of established data. The aim will be to steer the debate to the constructive and the positive. Should a special interest group be involved, it may not be too amenable to discussion and continue to view matters in terms of black and white. Then it is that the argument is directed so that the authorities and the wider public audience, the ultimate arbitrator, can be brought to see matters in perspective.

The world timber trade is working along these lines. The International Tropical Timber Organisation is a forum for discussion of the complex of interests of both consuming and producer countries and of the trade. These interests have to face conservation groups that, with growing success, are calling for restrictions and boycotts, to protect both what are seen as vulnerable resources *per se* and an environment essential to the survival of fauna and flora and indigenous tribes.

The result is a plan for labelling timber, to identify produce from soundly managed forests and countries with recognized ecological programmes. Definitions and verification processes still present difficulties in the way of full implementation of the scheme but all those involved have learned to communicate, both with each other and the outside world.

Reassurance for the employees

Often forgotten when all attention is focused on a public issue is the domestic situation. The morale of the workforce deserves better than to be left to the chance of enlightenment by the public media or outsider views. Anodyne circulars, appearing late into a controversy and simply reprinting management's known claims and viewpoint, are no substitute for a positive staff reassurance programme.

Managed communication sets out to expose the issues in full and not the positive alone (if only defensively, in recognition of the fact that matters cannot be fudged too much with people who are themselves at least partially involved). An adult and reasoned explanation of the situation proves the corporation has full confidence in its position and in the staff. The reward will be support and possibly direct help with individual contacts, even in cases where mistakes and inadvertent misjudgment have to be admitted.

It is salutary for a management locked in an adversarial conflict to monitor the internal perceptions, if only to see how far the desired message is being accepted by the workforce. It takes a tough mind to undertake such a study but the findings can bring a sense of perspective into an atmosphere that is likely to be heated by indignation and self-righteousness. Employees told of their value by the chairperson in his or her annual report cannot then be ignored at the most critical of times. See Figure 12.1.

	Attack		Defence
P R E S S U R E S	Protests	**C O M M U N I C A T E**	Full analysis
	Demands		Honest history
	Mistakes		Market monitor
			Trade support
	Aim		**Action**
	Controls		Public debate
	Prohibition		Staff consultation
	New law		Lobbyist
			Trade support

Figure 12.1 Environment battleground.

HANDLING THE REGULATORY FRAMEWORK

Regulatory issues are always with us: proposed new legislation, amendments to existing regulations, pleas for support and help are part of the day-to-day routine. The law establishes the operating framework but also changes as circumstances alter and even an apparently simple regulatory move, such as a revised standard, can have far-reaching implications.

Very large corporations maintain their own permanent links and deal directly with the authorities. The majority of companies, however, rely on their trade associations to make representations, monitor what is happening and to guard their interests generally. This liaison is part of the remit of the communication portfolio holder.

There is clear advantage to maintaining a sound link with the trade body and the industry generally, and making the task one for a senior director. The strength of a representative body, the respect it commands, is a direct function of the support it receives from the membership. A body known to be representative will be allowed entry and a hearing. The personal sympathy of the experienced professionals who man the trade association is a great help in times of crisis.

Crisis apart, it is useful routine to pay attention to the perceptions of the trade body. There may be hints of threatening squalls ahead and, in general, information and data that can usefully be fed into the planning process. Product managers, operating units, designers and researchers should all be made aware of industry thinking, an added perspective to the view of what is likely to lie ahead, of foreseen change.

The global market

International operations complicate the environmental communication task but differences in legal and regulatory requirements of markets also offer opportunities. This is particularly true in the field of taxation: the adjustment of operations to take advantage of allowances and provisions in the various markets can make a significant difference to overall results.

The communication challenge is to ensure that the corporation is capturing the data necessary to operational decision-making, on investment incentives, export enhancement programmes, the currency outlook, of in-market developments. Whether or not the in-house returns and reports are judged sufficient, managed communication invests in direct research and also monitors the data made available by the trade associations and published by governments.

The material is fed into the central databases by topic, product and country, is presented to the relevant groups, circulated directly and perhaps published in summary form by the in-house newsletters. Every element of the business is continually made aware of the changing environment and remains conscious of the need to check plans and programmes against the best available intelligence of what is happening.

COMMUNICATION AND THE FINANCIAL WORLD

Communication with the financial community is a continuous requirement, not confined only to times of need. Then it is likely to be difficult to forge links. Personal assessment and reputation are important in building the confidence that creates financial links and there is a clear advantage to maintaining this element of the network in good order.

The banks

Every enterprise has some financial links, if only with the local bank, in which case it is as well to maintain a level of personal contact. The periodic face-to-face conversation is usually welcomed.

The larger the enterprise, the more the contact with banks and financiers. The communication initiative then comes from both sides, the business needing advice and facilities, the banks offering additional services. Businesses are advised in all the literature to talk over affairs periodically with their bankers and not only when difficulties appear. It is helpful to put the financial houses on the newsletter circulation list and to arrange periodic presentations exposing them to current plans and progress. Being known and understood by the financial world is an important element in building a favourable environment for the business and the area features prominently on the communication checklist of links requiring continuous contact.

The financial markets

Most concerns of a given size maintain communication links with the financial markets. Apart from cash requirements, advice can be of advantage in any number of situations, acquisitions, mergers and cooperative arrangements, for which there may be only limited, if any, in-house expertise.

These links are maintained by the finance director but in the managed communication environment, in cooperation with the communication portfolio. Both executives are involved in the routine briefings given to financial analysts and the media on the outlook for the current period, to explain new ventures and major developments. Public companies have a strong interest in seeing their shares correctly assessed and valued by the bourse.

The information given to the financial markets is also made available to the workforce and staff. They are not left to discover from the media the outlook for the activities on which their livelihood depends. Many of the workforce have no contact with the financial pages and only receive reports of dubious accuracy third-hand on what is published there.

There is the timing difficulty. An afternoon briefing to catch the next day's press cannot be published internally in advance to every office. Nevertheless, a summary of what has been said can be faxed after the event, for display on all noticeboards that evening and on the following day. Subsequently, the information is repeated and expanded via the other media of the network. The staff are given proof that management is concerned to have everyone fully involved with the fortunes of the enterprise.

The shareholders

The links between a public company and its shareholders are laid down by law but it is common practice to do more than the minimum. The statutory annual report is supplemented by quarterly statements, important developments are announced independently as these occur (this is a legal requirement in the US) and, on occasion, visits to facilities are arranged.

However, it cannot be claimed that matters are satisfactory, that shareholders in general feel comfortable with what they are told and is revealed to the public.

The pressure for improved communication continues. Share ownership has to a significant degree passed from individuals to institutions, pension schemes, trusts and investment funds, and, while directors must be careful not to discriminate between shareholders, all being equal in law, the professional managers are coming to expect higher level and more detailed information than has been the rule.

An important feature is for top executives to run 'road show' presentations for institutional investors, to discuss prospects and answer queries. More important to fuller disclosure is the pressure on the accountancy professions for both clearer definitions and more standardized practices. The whole area is one of continuing controversy. Meanwhile, critics frequently claim to expose hidden features in the accounts of leading companies that raise questions as to the level of disclosure in the reported results.

Fraud apart, there is no agreement in sight to many aspects of accounting but communication has failed if the accounts become subject to controversy and a matter for investor concern. There is no need for it to happen.

The annual report and shareholder meeting, the primary financial communication channel for a public company, is given obvious care and attention. In normal circumstances, the aim is to communicate confidence in the business and its future prospects, specifically while in the care of the competent team to be seen up there on the top table.

Managed communication with shareholders does not begin and end with the annual meeting and the quarterly statements. However, research polls still report that directors 'have little time for private shareholders'. One published result was that only 5% of corporate directors of communication believe that feedback from shareholders is 'good value'. There is reportedly little respect for the 'aunt and uncle' attendance at meetings and no concern that these are people who help build brand loyalty and can have political impact.

The workforce

The workforce also has an interest. The annual report is available but not often actively promoted internally. There is also an unfortunate assumption that a presentation prepared for the public, and to meet legal requirements, is equally suitable and satisfactory for the staff. There are legal restrictions on what can be said but some further amplification and explanation, perhaps only a few extra paragraphs from the chairman, can enhance the document as a domestic communication tool.

A ritual sentence or two, in which the chairman acknowledges the contribution of the workforce during the past difficult year, does not show a heightened awareness of the communication function. As with the planning and budget cycle, the directors have a responsibility to communicate the year's results to the employees and this is best done by direct presentation. The 'show' created for, and mounted at the annual meeting can be equally displayed at meetings with the work-force.

The currency markets

An important link of the communication network for any but purely domestic operations is the monitor of currency movements. Hedging against future costs or to protect potential profit can make a significant difference to results. The function is one under the control of the chief financial officer but there continue to be lapses and even major corporations (such as Shell and Volkswagen) report large losses arising from control shortcomings.

A developed communication function ensures that currency and relevant transactions are recorded, e.g. entered in a restricted-access management database. Senior managers are then all aware, and known to be so, of what is being done.

COMMUNICATION MANAGEMENT OF DISASTER

Disaster strikes at any time. Sooner or later, the corporation will face a product failure, there will be an accident, or disaffected staff or malign outside interests will launch an attack on methods and practices. Worst of all, there can be a massive environmental breakdown.

These occasions test the maturity of the management and the strength of the corporate structure as a whole, but overcoming the crisis will depend on communication.

Physical disasters apart, a managed communication network is designed to give some warning of an impending storm. Direct complaints, whispers from the trade, technical assessments, will hint at a problem before the news hits the street. There will have been time to collect the facts, make assessments and to be prepared to respond positively, and perhaps to have started with remedial action.

Unfortunately, advance awareness cannot be taken for granted and, with that fact recognized, a disaster procedure is built into the network.

First reaction to disaster

First step of the disaster procedure is to establish responsibility for the handling of the affair or incident at the outset, at the moment of notification. This will:

- identify who is to be informed, the people to be called and consulted;
- set out the scope of initial response. There will be a guideline for handling the media, recognizing that a thoughtless comment or denial at the outset can magnify the problem and prolong an affair beyond reason.

The 'normal' disaster

Fortunately, most disasters are confined to one product or a place and do not threaten to destroy the organization. However, without a plan or documented procedure, response can be piecemeal and reactive to rather than seeking to lead developments.

When Johnson & Johnson, the world health care corporation, faced a blackmail threat to a major product, the reported poisoning of a household medicine, the company immediately took charge of the situation, 'went public' in the media with all the facts. As a result, public confidence was maintained and the damage contained.

Less happy was the experience of Dow Corning, another world corporation, and one that in fact had an elaborate product-monitor system based on reports and committees. Nevertheless, the company was caught unawares, or at least communicated confusion when the safety of silicone breast implants was questioned. It became clear subsequently that there had been muddle, with each step in the monitor system believing that responsibility lay elsewhere. In effect, a system existed but had not been reviewed and, when the crunch came, communication failed. Later the company took decisive action, explained what had happened and withdrew from the market but not without suffering considerable damage and legal claims running on for years.

A classic case of floundering into destruction was that of the A.H. Robins company. For a decade, the company's management reacted to concerns about its Dalkon Shield product by attacking critics and even the judiciary. The damage proved irreparable and the company was driven into bankruptcy.

Dealing with an essentially minor problem, but one that has caught the public eye, makes an extortionate call on top management time. Allegations by a disaffected employee that have caught media attention are an example of a not infrequent scenario, one usually based on the reportedly dubious sales and marketing practices of a multinational. Invariably there will have been internal complaints and an unhappy situation in the affected operating unit but clearly management has not been alerted. The fault then lies with a failure in communication, the network has been allowed to deteriorate.

In such an unguarded situation, an updated disaster plan will still prove more than justified in saving some of the agony and cost. There will be an established, possibly tested procedure: specifically, someone will take responsibility immediately for coping with the affair and for initiating the investigative process. There will be a guideline for the professional handling of the media and the authorities, if they also become involved. Events move fast in a crisis and there is no time to start from the beginning and think out a programme for dealing effectively with a problem after it 'breaks'. Hesitancy and the mistakes it breeds can prove expensive.

Worst-scene disaster

Computer systems have been developed to stimulate worst-scene disasters such as a major oil spill or a factory explosion. The executive team is given an opportunity to handle a situation in the light of typical reactions from the authorities, on the stock exchanges or in the media. One early lesson is that, as with a 'normal' difficulty, the unprepared can actually make a situation worse.

It has been suggested that corporations vulnerable to major catastrophe, particularly those in transport, chemicals and oil, should hold regular crisis rehearsals for the management team. However, given the realities of organizational life, the personnel changes, travel, preoccupation in the routine, this is but a partial answer. 'Training' requires the back-up of a step-by-step disaster plan which charts responsibility for collecting information, coordinating the expert and technical resources, for handling legal implications and communicating with the media and public.

A plan needs periodic review and this is perhaps best done formally at some stage in the annual planning cycle. When the unthinkable does happen, there is some comfort in having a workable guide at hand, avoiding panic and holding the organization together. Key points will include specifying the stage at which the chief executive is called to take over personally, the handling of the media and obtaining legal advice. The staff, important suppliers or the trade are natural allies and, if kept directly informed, can be rallied in support.

Two examples illustrate the extremes. It took great pressure from the US authorities for the Firestone company to recall its 500 series radial tyres in 1978. There had been some 14 000 consumer complaints but the company continued to maintain confidence in the product until the publicity seriously damaged its market and sales.

In contrast, the Perrier water company immediately took the product off the shelves worldwide when its purity was questioned, ran a full and open publicity campaign and clearly set out to retain public confidence. It has evidently succeeded in doing so.

Blunders

Unsuspected blunders can hit the most experienced operator, on a scale so massive as to threaten continued existence. A Pepsi Cola promotion in the Philippines promised a cash prize for certain numbered bottle tops but went on to print the wrong number, leaving many consumers frustrated when they were unable to claim. Not even the world resources of the corporation could have met the theoretical costs, and the company, some of whose personnel were physically attacked, lost the market.

In the UK, the Hoover appliance manufacturer suffered substantial loss financially and in reputation through a promotion that offered free air tickets with every purchase over a relatively low minimum. The organization could not cope with the overwhelming response. The company then compounded the damage by appearing to be seeking to limit its exposure – 'by a degree of indecision and a denial of the magnitude of the problem', in the words of one commentator. The effect on individual careers apart, the cost of the disaster was such as to affect the parent corporation.

Pepsi had a very unfortunate accident but in the case of Hoover the marketing plan was not linked into a communication network, was not open to general review and discussion. Neither corporation appeared to have had a plan or policy guidelines for dealing with disaster.

Documentation

The existence of documentation setting out expected behaviour and standards, in each relevant office and published in the policy manual, is in itself useful to counter an attack or investigation. Whatever the shortcomings of an individual, of misguided decisions, here it can be pointed out, are the governing rules, published and widely available.

Unfortunate action may have been taken under the stress of circumstances but the corporation has loftier principles, standards that can be shown to have applied for years past. The policy manual itself is proof that the standards have been communicated, that the intention to maintain them and operate accordingly is serious. All concerned understand their responsibilities.

Increasingly, too, corporations are publishing statements of their business practices and ideals. One of the world's largest communication companies, British Telecom, notes its commitment to rewarding **shareholders** and keeping them 'well informed'; promises suppliers to make 'full and fair' use of its purchasing powers; and tells **employees** that they will be treated with 'fairness and respect'.

Addressing the wider public, BT promises to 'support the social, economic and cultural well-being of the **communities** in which it does business ... have an environmental policy ... and publish an annual environmental report recording our targets and our achievements'.

A certain cynicism can greet such statements but the fact is that they do communicate aims and intentions which the policy-makers cannot avoid taking into account in the day-to-day management of the business. In turn, there develops a (perhaps only partly conscious) way of doing things, of working practices. In the case of BT, there can be no doubt that it has achieved a status that would have been unthinkable a decade earlier.

BUILDING RELATIONSHIPS

The suppliers

Contact with suppliers is an important element of managed communication. In normal times, suppliers are competing for the business but inevitably the occasion arises when the company will look to its sources for support, perhaps for an extension of credit, an extra specification or a special delivery. Suppliers are also an important source of market intelligence.

Suppliers deserve recognition as partners in the always difficult task of building and running a business. Managed communication provides for contact between customer and supplier over and above the terms of trade. Much of this will be personal but suppliers are kept informed of plans and the outlook, possibly directly by more formal review and also by being included on the circulation list of house newsletters.

Effort put into communication with suppliers is repaid in full, not only in terms of extra service but also by way of information. Suppliers are in touch with the industry at levels not open to a principal and can be the conduit for data and intelligence available through no other source.

The trade association

A strong trade association helps both to build links with the marketplace and to monitor change, and also gives the assurance of strength in the face of common problems. Competition laws are strict but do not prevent members of an industry communicating in pursuit of legitimate interests, such as taking a common stand on legislation or keeping alert to global events and terms of trade. An active trade body is consulted by the authorities and in turn makes representations, forging connections with officials and politicians that are beyond the capacity of an individual company.

A good trade organization also works on communication with the public at large, producing films and educational materials, making available speakers and arranging special events to promote its industry. A criticism of such effort is that the measure of 'success' in part lies in the eye of the sponsor, while the disinterested public continues on its unheeding way. Nevertheless, trade promotional effort is doubtless noticed by officials and opinion leaders, and by immediate customers. Such results alone makes industry campaigns worth considering.

Communication with local communities

Managed communication recognizes the value of building sound relations with local communities. Common techniques include direct sponsorship of local occasions, donations and support for events and charities.

Large corporations have world guidelines for the purpose but even a local enterprise can support the hospital, the town theatre or the sports team, possibly by an imaginative and memorable donation in kind rather than cash. The satisfaction of being appreciated apart, local goodwill can have more direct benefit, by attracting sympathetic listeners, perhaps even support, in times of difficulty, e.g. for a planning action or in a disagreement with the authorities.

The farming lobbies are an outstanding example of the value of community communication, keeping public opinion supportive of subsidy and protection on an unprecedented and continuing basis. On a smaller scale, but no less vocal, arts interests have succeeded in communicating the value of their activities to gain substantial support from the taxpayer. The arts are not cohesive but elements, notably opera, dance and some theatre, have successfully learned the two-way pattern of communication, first 'listening' – in effect guiding opinion, and then building the argument of their case for public support.

Unnumbered social organizations (there are over 250 000 charities registered in the UK alone) clamour for official and private help. In the normal course of events, a group is born on a wave of support for a cause that has caught the imagination of the times but then continued existence necessitates professional organization and communication.

Enthusiasm wanes, new issues arise and the established groups have to adapt to survive. The focus of animal charities, for instance, has altered from one of protection and the prevention of certain cruelties to the safeguarding of overall 'rights'. On the other hand, many charities have not adapted and today little is heard of such societies as those against alcohol, or propagating specific religious aims, in contrast to those seeking to raise the living standards of the poorer countries of the world.

Community communication has become highly professional, reaching well beyond the purely commercial aim of establishing neighbourhood goodwill.

SUMMARY

Managed communication monitors and seeks to develop constructive dialogue with environmental and special interest groups. The function is attuned to the regulatory climate.

The basis is 'listening' to ensure early awareness of developments or concerns and then having the discipline to analyse and face a situation. The inherent value of even destructive 'opposition' is recognized.

The staff, suppliers and related industrial interests are seen as natural allies.

Communication with the financial world is a special assignment for a senior executive, cooperating with the communication portfolio holder. Employees are kept as informed at the same level as is the market.

Managed communication maintains and updates contingency plans for coping with disaster, both the catastrophic and the more 'normal', such as the product failure, a mistake or a public attack. The existence of documentation, published in the policy manual, proves useful in countering criticism and meeting the queries of investigators.

The communication network also embraces the local communities in which an enterprise operates, seeking to build goodwill and support for the operation.

REFERENCES

1. Nader, R. (1965) *Unsafe at Any Speed*, Grossman; Carson, R. (1963) *Silent Spring*, Hamish Hamilton, London, UK.
2. Rifkin, J. (1994) *Beyond Beef*, Thorson.

13

TOOLS FOR COMMUNICATION

Market research, public relations and advertising are tools of the communication network. Their successful employment is based on the communication brief. The communicator is required to understand both the scope and the limitations of these professional disciplines.

INTRODUCTION

The three professional tools continuously employed by the communicator are:

- **Market research** A great range of techniques is used to study the existing market, investigate the untapped or potential market and to forecast the future. Market Research is also valuable in the assessment of the in-house situation.
- **Public relations** A conduit for carrying information to and influencing the market and environment but also a skill employed in the assessment and analysis of current status and change. Public relations have a useful internal role.
- **Advertising** The continuing effort to inform and motivate, to communicate effectively with the market.

These functions of the marketing programme are integral elements of the communication network. Their employment is not spasmodic, only being called upon as a need appears to arise, but part of the planned and budgeted annual cycle. Other marketing elements are dependent on the network for market knowledge and the monitoring of needs and change, but are not directly linked to the communicator. Design and quality, for instance, communicate a powerful message but it is one that is built into and is intrinsic in the product itself.

The successful use of the professional marketing disciplines lies in the quality of the briefing given to the practitioners. The better the brief, the better the research and the advertisement. The preparation of a full and actionable brief is a key communication skill.

MARKET RESEARCH

The existing or established market

The communicator uses market research continuously to maintain contact with and monitor every aspect of the existing market. The programme will quantify and identify demand on the **5W** principle of communication:

- **W**ho is buying: the buyer or consumer profile by every relevant feature of age, income, residence, interest and need.
- **W**hat is being purchased: by model, size, colour, and also of competitive products or systems. Consumption will be measured by population segment.
- **W**hen sales occur: many markets are seasonal but when is the buying decision made? In sectors such as clothing and toys, product planning and trade buying is well ahead of the peak consumption periods and manufacturers, the trade, retail outlets all have different time scales in the chain of demand. Patterns vary: holiday-makers in Britain tend to book well in advance whereas Italians are more likely to decide what they wish to do nearer the time – and these patterns differ by age and the other consumer characteristics.
- **W**here the sales are being made, leading in turn to assessment of the distribution systems to ensure these remain optimal.
- **W**hy the purchases are being made, of own and competitive products and, again, identified by the various categories of consumers.

The potential market

Understandably, much of the attention is devoted to the established market and to existing competition but the untapped potential cannot be ignored. If 70% of the population uses supermarkets (as is shown by some estimates) it is unwise of the operators not to wonder, and seek to find out, what the remaining 30% are doing and why they are acting in the way they do. Looking at the 'non-market' can reveal serious gaps in service, in failure to meet need, and open the very opportunity sought by the entrepreneurial competitor.

The history of retailing in particular, is based on exploitation of the 'non-market', with new channels of supply over-taking established, unchanged methods. The apparently dominant food supermarkets, for instance, face the challenge in both the USA and Europe of operations that meet a demand for streamlined outlets able to operate more economically and offer lower prices.

While much intelligence on the existing market can and is built up from internal data and the reporting system, a clear view of the 'non-market' can only be established by professional research. The potential or 'non-market' has also to be viewed in terms of the **5W** principle: **w**ho are the people/customers not buying currently; **w**hy not and **w**hat are they buying; **w**hen and ho**w** are they likely to develop, or be persuaded to recognize a need, become approachable; and **w**here are the non-buyers located?

Forecasting

Forecasting the future, projecting current trends beyond the immediate budget or plan is a major task for the market researcher. An understood feature of the forecast is that, to a greater or lesser extent, the result will be inaccurate and even badly wrong.

This fact does not invalidate the effort put into forecasting; it is simply a factor to be recognized and accepted as part of the operational environment. Without a forecast and a vision of the future, planning is meaningless. Production capacity, distribution systems, research and development are elements that typically require long lead times and have to be geared to meeting accepted objectives. There has to be a plan.

In an environment of managed communication, updating the vision and reforecasting will be on a regular basis, allowing the enterprise to adjust to changing conditions. In practice, it will not be feasible, for instance, to cancel a major facility halfway through construction simply because some perceptions have changed. Nevertheless, reforecasting helps both to build flexibility into the system and to keep attention focused on reality.

The market forecast with a discussion of the latest update are valuable links in the communication network, available on the terminals and in hard copy format. Every element of planning is given a common purpose and, as the view alters, is encouraged to make adjustments in unison.

The hazards of data assessment

Market research is growing in sophistication as electronic capabilities continue to refine techniques, allow the capture of ever-increasing volumes of data and speed the delivery of intelligence. National political polling is carried out in a matter of hours. The accurate monitor of sales and consumption does not lag far behind, and assessments of consumer opinions and beliefs can also be undertaken quickly. These data are aligned to any desired demographic profile.

The availability of accurate and clearly-defined information sustains success. On occasion, it is success itself, perhaps most famously when Rothschild arranged for advanced communication on the outcome of the battle of Waterloo – and made an immediate fortune.

Clearly, data cannot replace inspiration and intuition but intelligence does provide a foundation for, and then runs in parallel with creativity. At the outset, the start of a business, the entrepreneur and the communicator are possibly one and the same person; no matter how affairs develop subsequently, the two functions remain closely linked.

While the utility of market research is no longer questioned, the function does have its limitations. Users of quantitative data need to have some understanding of statistics and their interpretation in the light of sampling and probability theory. In the collection of qualitative information, the questioning of people, the design of the questionnaire, is always difficult and both the professional researcher and the user must learn to restrain enthusiasm and work only with material that can be shown to be reliable.

The questionnaire

Given the ubiquity of electronic data handling, few questionnaires are 'open-ended', that is allowing the respondent to answer in his or her own words. The material is then too difficult to code and format into standard data. There are various alternatives. One popular technique is to have respondents choose one or more points from a list of attributes. The difficulty is that none of these may correspond exactly to the individual's view or if there is too long a list of choices, answer fatigue sets in and the replies become careless.

An example of the difficulties of interviewing occurred during one crisis, when the pollster asked if the respondent would support war and, if so, whether this would continue to be the case should there be 100 or 500 casualties. To all intents and purposes, as the question was given no context, it was meaningless, e.g. no consideration was given to the implications of surrender or any other factor.

There is difficulty in questioning the disinterested, e.g. to ask for ratings of insurance services of people who, for whatever reason, have given no thought to the subject for many years. In order to meet the criteria of the statistical design, the pollster continues nevertheless, but the actual material gathered from such interviews could well mislead and, at best, can have but little value.

To quote some of the discussion:

> Current questionnaire design seems to rely on predicting all possible answers to a question and not allowing for any new ideas or expressions from the respondents. This is further reinforced by giving the acceptable answers to respondents in a large proportion of questions ... Much attitude research is based on formal batteries of attitude statements with answer scales provided to respondents ... Many of the words we use in questionnaires seem to be relatively uncommon or potentially ambiguous or problem words ... we are probably introducing a whole range of error into our measurements ...

> Only around one-third of market research questions aim to collect the 'harder' sorts of data associated with facts, past behaviour and current behaviour. Well over half are trying to measure the much 'softer' issues of attitudes, opinions or belief ...

> There is a huge body of evidence to support the claim that changing question-wording will change the results. The examples range from deliberate attempts to introduce bias, to observations of the effects of trivial changes to a single word or phrase ...

> The continual quest for the right question, for the correct wording, for lack of bias and non-leading wording was the essence of

good questionnaire design. But the lingering doubts remain: if everyone is an expert, or if several experts disagree, then what is the right question? How do you decide? Which version best measures the truth?

An example: the accepted wording for questioning holiday trends was '4 nights or more away from home' until a test showed that many people actually heard the phrase as 'fortnight or more' (John O'Brien).[1]

Clearly, even 'listening' is complex and all data has to be handled cautiously, assessed in the light of the parameters used and the definitions.

Caution with interpretation

The professional researcher works in a competitive environment, with clients seeking more information and requiring that it be built on data that are more accurate, dependable and specific.

Given the charged atmosphere, and spurred on to be different and innovative, the researcher is tempted to step beyond the professional role of collecting and analysing data, to go on and offer 'solutions' to the client's 'problems'. Since information on attitudes and behaviour cannot be absolute and interpretations vary, researchers see themselves as neutral and unbiased and are tempted to present data in terms of conclusions, the 'results' of studies as specifics for action.

The presentation of study results is expected from them and forms part of the brief but in acting as interpreters, researchers are to be seen but as an outside analyst. The communicator will also want to see the actual findings, the 'raw data', and to study the techniques employed. Experience and flair are important determinants in the use of data, a point not often stressed in the textbooks nor, it must be said, by the researcher in presenting the findings. Obtaining exciting insight for a new product from young housewives does not help if the real market is to be the pensioner.

The researcher stimulates thinking, suggests possibilities based on much experience, but in the final analysis, it is study of the material, of completed questionnaires and tapes of interviews, that might provide insights obvious to the principal alone.

An example that makes the point was the research into a new

market that showed a clear preference for one brand. The research report discussed this leading brand's advantages in terms of effectiveness, price, etc. However, examination of the data showed regular reference to the actual bottle and enquiry with the local agent quickly revealed that the container was ideal for a storage need in that country. The recommended plan, with its segmentation analysis and updated packaging, would have been a total failure; an experienced executive, checking the original data, was able to avoid the loss of a bad mistake.

Equally, the 'raw data' can reveal opportunity, a market or niche not currently supplied. The alert communicator who identified, in surveys of the advertising industry, the need for a specialist and 'neutral' media time and space-buying service, went on to establish a substantial business in France and then elsewhere.

A summary of the impact of professional communication tools is given in Table 13.1.

Table 13.1 Summary of the impact of professional communication tools

	Internal use	*External activity*
Market research	Market results Market structure and motivation Proposal tests Staff views	—
Public relations	House material Policy explanation Market monitor	Media contact Direct activity Creating climate
Advertising	—	Market campaigns

THE DATA EXPLOSION

The explosion of information on markets is bringing ever closer the 'ideal': continuous contact with each individual customer, the monitor at the store checkout, the lifestyle assessment in the home, on holiday, at the doctor's.

An example lies in health care. While the doctor is not the consumer of drugs, it is through his prescribing activity that medicines are sold.

The manufacturers of pharmaceuticals run extensive programmes to collect and maintain detailed records on every practitioner, of his or her specialities and other interests, of availability and receptiveness to sales-people, of the personal and practice profile. When the representative calls, it is possible to target the visit to the known interests of the doctor.

The data also allow messages, via the mail, electronically and even over dedicated radio wavebands, to be personalized. Special events, such as seminars and symposia, are carefully geared to the known interests of the health specialist groups.

The suppliers of major capital goods also seek personal acquaintance to guide them through the maze of committee and approval pro-cedures. Here communication is not simply person-to-person but involves spectrums of people, the direct negotiators and their associ-ates, financiers and banks, diplomats and government ministers. At this point, market research begins to give way to public relations.

A hazard in too much data

A hazard of the information explosion is the distraction of good-to-know material, data that is interesting but has little if any direct bear-ing on issues and objectives.

The great mass of data available to the travel industry, for instance, is all interesting: the numbers of travellers, reasons for being on the move, preferred times, required facilities and any number of sub- and cross-analyses all look meaningful. However, any one interest, an hotel, a resort, a tour operator or a carrier, does not have the resources to study all this material and even if it had, would find that in the indi-vidual circumstances, only a fraction of the information would be actionable and of use in meeting objectives.

Leading hotels in Frankfurt or Rome can do little with data showing how many Americans are travelling to Europe this season. What would be usable is knowledge, and it would need to be by income bracket and interests, of where the travellers originate. Then it would be possi-ble to communicate with them in their home cities.

The communicator seeks the relevant and actionable. Routine deliv-ery of a mass of figures can lead to the bored dismissal of the data, a failure to identify and grasp the significant facts. When a crisis looms there is no time to start searching back files and data banks for relevant information. In using market research, communication management aims to ensure that the format and presentation of data is reviewed, critically assessed on a regular basis, and from the user standpoint.

THE FULL EMPLOYMENT OF PUBLIC RELATIONS

Much of public relations is concerned with routine, the preparation of publicity and media material, the organization of events, the running of sponsorships. The function is also in part reactive. An organization of any size needs a mechanism or channel for dealing with outside inquiries, from the media, shareholders, officials (perhaps from customers where this is not a sales responsibility). Top management cannot be available to order nor, necessarily, are the senior people best able to deal with ad hoc inquiries and the day-to-day routine of outside contact.

The sophisticated use of public relations, to influence opinion, create a sympathetic climate, involves the subtle building of contact via every channel of communication and the personal persuasion of those identified as opinion leaders. Given managed communication, public relations also has a responsibility for feedback, to assist in the assessment of the market and the monitor of change. Public relations contacts, targeted to the achievement of specific objectives, are not necessarily representative in the statistical sense. Nevertheless, the information obtained by PR activity provides a subjective balance to the structured, objective view presented by market research.

The public relations reports synthesis opinion, including those of the public media, quote the views of individuals, perhaps gathered by way of private contact, and flesh out the bare figures and facts of market research and internal data.

In turn, this added depth of understanding builds into a programme for the use of public relations to meet identified objectives, to communicate with the market and the wider environment in parallel with the advertising and promotional campaigns. In this way the communication network uses public relations as an integral element of the annual cycle, not simply as a specialist department called in on the basis of need, or to meet a specific situation.

Sponsorship

Successful sponsorship requires a professional approach, with identified aims and a workable programme. It is one thing for an important oil company to support opera and have this acknowledged in the publicity, recognized as an enlightened contribution to the community.

In contrast it is perhaps ostentatious for a regional brewery to sponsor a national exhibition, announce its 'continued commitment to the development of the arts ... demonstrate our ability to keep pace with current social issues' and go on to mention fine products which are totally unknown outside its area (and not available even at the exhibition refreshment centre).

In the marketplace, the desired image is built and carefully fostered by speaking to known target segments, using a message coordinated at the centre but carefully local in approach. A corporate style, running through all the media, from letterhead to the promotional campaigns, helps to make the impact but language and implementation is local and in the current idiom. Even the best of translations read and sound discordant.

The public media

In-market activity is built on authenticated local perceptions: the novel idea or theme, whether developed locally or imported from success elsewhere, is used only after testing. Time spent in checking for racial and cultural differences is seldom wasted and saves the anguish and pain that follows the insensitive, ignorant handling of affairs.

Coca-Cola has historically had great success with this approach, a notable example being the corporation's world song, a central theme well adapted around the globe. On the other hand, it is not difficult to find disasters, where word or design has caused dissent, even uproar.

The 'experts', agents, consultants and long-established residents, are to be heard with a degree of scepticism. The business executive who would not take his own views or those of a few colleagues, however experienced, as representative of the home market, needs to guard against basing 'export' market activity on the opinion of the agent or local manager alone. Managed communication accords every market the respect given to the home country with action based on professional market research and public relations assessment.

In the marketplace

The local businessman, the small professional practice, the town theatre, all communicate with their market on a daily basis, participate in community activity, follow neighbourhood interests in seeking an image which attracts and holds custom. Talking to the marketplace is being sympathetic to the housewife in the local shop as much as striving for recognition on the national and even the world stage. However, the public and the market are selfish, most of all with time and attention. Successful public relations is built on recognition of the fact that audiences are won and held when the perceived self-interest of the individual is clearly addressed.

Information and news that the announcer believes should be of interest, ought to be known by the public, will be lost in the general noise. The world continues on its oblivious daily round unless its own concerns are recognized and addressed.

To proclaim that 'we are pleased to announce the formation of our new company ... offer our new X, Y, Z services ... are planning other exciting facilities and please contact us' is generally to talk to the deaf. An alternative approach, perhaps to pick out the benefits of one service, to offer a trial on special terms, creates interest and adds excitement to the marketplace.

The annual report

Among the deadest of communications can be one of the most important, the statement of the president or chairman in the **annual report**. Sometimes this is even used to ascend the Olympian heights and to call for reform, perhaps of the related environment but even on occasion of the world order of things.

Annual reports are a tempting but poor medium for august pronouncements. Professional public relations advice would be that the message is unlikely to reach those targeted while diluting the primary purpose, impacting the shareholders. It is necessary on occasion to 'go public' on a specific problem faced by a company or industry but sensitivity to potential reaction can lead to the message being massaged by several people, even in committee. The result then is anodyne and characterless.

The difficulty can be overcome by identification of the purpose, what the chairman is seeking to achieve. If the aim is technical, making a professional case, the approach will differ from an attempt to influence the public at large. Trying to do both at once confuses the issue.

Image building

Specific tasks apart, a prime function of public relations is to build and maintain a favourable image for the enterprise. This can be an amorphous objective, with available resources disappearing down a bottomless pit.

The benefits of a positive image are clear but given limits to what can be done, there has to be a decision on priorities. Perhaps the first need can be identified as improved relations with the financial markets, or the achievement of a legislative change. More broadly, the aim might be to become recognized as pre-eminent in a given field or in underlining environmental care despite hazardous operation, but whatever the case, to be useful, a public relations programme requires a clear directive from management.

The formulation of the directive is in itself a valuable element of the annual planning cycle. It is part of top management's re-examination of the basic 'where are we ... and ... where are we going?' question. It is in this process that executives are expected to face up to the adverse, both in the way of existing or potential opposition to what is proposed or to a specific project in the company's programme, and also to identified market and environmental change that poses tangible threats to the business.

It is a time for clear thinking, to eschew the temptation to fudge difficulties and to look honestly at what might be, or has already become questionable activity. The scope of what can be done to rectify matters might be limited in the short term but at least no one is fooled as to the true state of affairs and, if public or legal difficulties do arise, management is prepared and in a position to take a clear-headed view of the way ahead.

Managed communication has public relations as a continuing function: a helpful deed, an appreciated sponsorship or a supportive media notice is not remembered for long and the goodwill dissipates if not reinforced and underlined by further activity.

History illustrates the point well. Organizations dependent on public support and goodwill, such as those concerned with slavery, alcoholism or Christian observance, so dominant in Europe and America in the nineteenth century, today attract virtually no interest. Many in fact do continue to play a role but have failed to adapt and allowed themselves to stultify, to lose contact with the public. In contrast, charities seeking to alleviate suffering in Africa or to protect the world habitat, highly professional in the use of public relations and communication in general, have captured the public sympathy and won massive support.

ADVERTISING

The high visibility of advertising in the marketing programme ensures that much of communication management is devoted to the function. In the case of consumer goods, advertising is usually the main operational concern.

The development of a sound campaign starts with the brief. It is a truism that the better the brief, the better the resulting advertising, a fact well recognized by such global marketing leaders as Unilever. These organizations arrange specialist courses solely for the purpose of exposing their operational management to the art of briefing.

The advertising brief

The skeleton of the advertising brief is, again, the **5W** principle of communication, explaining:

- **w**ho is the consumer, the purchaser, the decision-maker; also described is the competition and what it is doing;
- **w**hat the need is that the product or service meets; perhaps it is simple usage of the item, or it is fulfilling a deeper need/satisfaction;
- **w**here the consumers are located or the point of purchase;
- **w**hen the purchases are made, the timing of the buying decision, the seasonal changes;
- **w**hy or **h**ow the consumer is motivated, the perceptions to which he or she responds, how it appears that these can be exploited.

The **5W** review is unending, beginning anew as each campaign is put in place and runs its course. Then follows the analysis of the degree of success achieved in reaching the target market, in gaining attention and in conveying the conviction that led to purchases or subscriptions. The causes of complete failure and the reasons for outstanding success are usually clear but the great majority of results fall in between and there is always a degree of uncertainty as to the reasons for a particular outcome. A communication skill is to get the analysis sufficiently right for it to become a good base for the next round.

Advertising policy

Each season or cycle, advertising policy has to be delineated. Campaigns can range from an effort to enhance corporate identity; more usually, to promote the products and services, and sometimes the aim is to 'knock', that is, attack a specific competitor. In parallel, there is always a new fashion in advertising, a current dogma or accepted insight. The communicator sees behind the jargon to assess and consider the proposals objectively.

An approach that can be admired by the professionals, gratify the creative mind and the agency, may have little to say to the consumer. Much of the challenge of managing advertising lies in this judgment of how best to attract and hold the consumer interest, the essential preliminary to any transaction.

Advertising policy has wider implications. Alfred P. Sloan, in *My Years with General Motors*, records how his corporation overtook Ford, with its policy of keeping to one fixed design, by deliberately diversifying and providing a car 'for every purse and every purpose'.[2] Part of the process was the setting up of an Institutional Advertising committee to coordinate the function and to ensure that campaigns had the approval of all concerned, that these were not simply the bright ideas of the professionals.

Sloan noted that 'even if it was assumed that the value of the advertising was negligible, the other benefits accruing to the Corporation by the development of a General Motors atmosphere and the working together spirit of all members of the committee representing the various phases of the Corporation's activities ... the cost was well justified'.

The communication management of advertising ensures:

- the development of a sound brief tied to the budget objectives;
- an approved policy for the scope and type of campaigning;
- general acceptance of and agreement to the programme, i.e. not of the product and marketing management alone but also of those, such as the sales teams, who are directly dependent on its success;
- the monitor and assessment of results achieved by each campaign;
- testing of alternative approaches, outside the scope of current activities, for promoting both the products and services and also in seeking contact with untouched market segments.

MAINTAINING THE INTERNAL NETWORK

The three functions, of market research, public relations and advertising, are also employed in maintaining the internal communication network.

A regular cycle of **research** measures the perceptions and aspirations of the workforce. In particular, the programme establishes whether matters important to the employees, the work practices and facilities, organization and training, are seen to be improving or declining. Also part of this internal 'listening' is the assessment of communication itself, that it is recognized as flowing up and down the organization, that everyone is conscious of a direct link into the system.

Occasionally, research will study a specific issue, an office move, new procedures, altered work patterns. The aim then is to ensure that reaction to the proposal is judged on a neutral, professional basis and not simply on ad hoc or unstructured discussion.

Public relations undertakes important elements of the internal communication function. The PR office edits the house magazine and newsletters, and cooperates with the personnel office in publicizing and explaining employment policies. Public relations helps to put across the management programme in general, encouraging everyone to identify with the common purpose.

Equally important is a public relations programme focused on the interface with the public, friendly reception at the front desk, helpful on the telephone, clearly knowledgeable and efficient at the sales point.

Albert Gubay, the founder of the Kwik-Save cut-price chain in the UK, who went on to achieve success in New Zealand and the USA, tells how, after several years of small-scale trading in north Wales, he went to his bank for a loan with which to launch his first store. The local town branch had insufficient authority and he was taken to the regional office where, on hearing of the plan, the director asked the local manager how many of the threatened established stores were customers of the bank. A week later Gubay was not only refused the loan but his existing facility was withdrawn with immediate effect.

Managed communication will not save a business from mistakes, perhaps not even from stupidity, but will create awareness of and seek to build diplomacy and tact into the system. There will be stress on the importance of the individual links, on the value placed on relationships.

UNDERCOVER RESEARCH AND ESPIONAGE

Modern surveillance techniques and sophisticated bugging devices are sometimes alleged to have lifted industrial and commercial espionage to the level of an industry. However, it must be doubtful if illegal tactics are as widespread as these reports, which seem to emanate largely from vested interests and security consultants, suggest.

Espionage would have to be extensive indeed to yield more intelligence than a well-managed company-wide communication network, linked to the market and in touch with suppliers, trade sources and the environment. Legality and morality apart, the question arises as to what additional information there is to be gathered that cannot be captured routinely.

It is interesting that the post-Cold War opening up of the vast Eastern bloc police files has revealed their data on millions of citizens to be largely trivial, misleading and even invented. The information on Western personalities has been seen to be less complete than that to be found in published references.

The atmosphere of espionage, the aura of illicit data, does not appear to be conducive to rational assessment, cool judgment. Undoubtedly, there are points of sensitivity, when knowledge of a price quote, of contract details, of a cost structure would be of real value but assessment and the exercise of judgment would seem to provide as good a basis for action as any. The only illicit bugging, during a takeover bid, experienced by the author, served but to illustrate how easy it is for such attempts to be bungled and discovered. Even so it was difficult to envisage what more data than that already available the 'spies' thought could be captured. Lack of judgment was the most likely cause of their defeat.

Conflict analysis

More sophisticated can be the effort to glean intelligence in the grey area between espionage and market research. Conflict analysis can identify the likely moves of existing competition and of other potential threats and there is a certain comfort in knowing how things stand, the likely moves of the competition.

One ploy is to arrange for attendance at seminars and events staged by rival organizations, to observe their techniques and market approach, discover how far matters are advanced. In serious situations, an attempt might be made to subvert or hire a key competitor employee or, less directly, seek information through social contact.

British Airways went to extraordinary lengths to obtain details of rival Virgin Airways' passengers but the strategy backfired when exposed and cost the company heavily in morale, prestige and also financially. Other cases come to light periodically but these usually appear in the guise of dirty tricks designed to secure a specific advantage.

There are consultants who specialize in the legitimate checking and

gathering of information on the competition. They will, for instance, analyse training programmes, sales force deployment, research capacity, to obtain further insight on what is planned or likely to be done – but this is, in effect, a dimension of the network of managed company-wide communication.

SUMMARY

Communication management builds the disciplines of market research, public relations and advertising into the network.

- **Market research** is used to 'listen' to the marketplace, reporting statistically on what is happening and also seeking the reasons 'why', the factors that motivate activity.

  Full use of market research implies an understanding both of the statistical methods employed and of interview techniques, and of the limitations of each. While welcoming the experience and interpretative abilities of the researcher, the communicator also studies the 'raw' data, searching for insight that direct experience might bring to light.
- **Public relations** is employed to maintain the routines of contact with the market. More broadly, the function is charged with the task of creating a climate of favourable opinion, both to achieve specific objectives and for the corporation as a whole.
- **Advertising** is the high-profile communication activity; for much of consumer industry it is the main tool. The emphasis is on the creativity and flair that will attract the attention of a noisy marketplace, but the foundation of successful contact is the quality of the brief. The **5W** principle of communication provides the skeleton around which the brief is built.
- **Internally**, all three skills are used to communicate with the workforce, to build and maintain the links between the network and each individual.
- **Espionage**, particularly by use of modern technology, has attracted attention but much of what is said to be done can perhaps be better described as the successful management of the communication network.

REFERENCES

1. O'Brien, J. (1987) *Journal of the Market Research Society (UK)*, **29**(3).
2. Sloan, A.P. (1963) *My Years with General Motors*, Orbit SA.

14

INTEGRATING THE PHYSICAL MEDIA OF COMMUNICATION

The physical media of communication range from the logo, developed once in a generation, to the humble noticeboard, changed daily. The two main media, electronic and print, continue to offer the communicator new opportunities.

INTRODUCTION

The historic means of communication, the spoken and the written, have been enhanced and augmented by the electronic, but the added capacity, and the new opportunities have further underlined the need for discrete management of the function. A network is built first on understanding and then making full and integrated use of every one of the media available.

THE LOGO

The logo, the all-embracing symbol, is created perhaps once in the life of a corporation, possibly to be amended by each succeeding generation. Even when long-established and familiar to the point of no longer being noticed by the habituated, the logo is and remains a powerful communicator. For the outside world it is a sign of recognition and stability; internally, the logo is a unifier, a common denominator. Proof of its value, if such were needed, lies in the attention devoted to, and often the expense of, any change.

Developing or changing the logo is not an easy exercise. Varying artistic appreciation apart, the symbol is a focus on purpose, the most concentrated expression of how the corporation or organization sees itself. Much hard and clear-headed thinking goes into its creation.

Once accepted, the logo is exploited by a detailed programme, expanding its use from the notepaper of head office to every point of visibility. A simple decision, to introduce the logo on all stationery, requires the issue of a manual, carrying detailed print specifications and examples of each mail item approved for use throughout the organization. It is a formidable task in one country, never mind worldwide.

The stationery is important but development of a logo implies a wider purpose, a recognition of the need for a unifying element. As such it can appear on buildings, on vehicles, in advertising, on the product itself, gaining recognition at every point of exposure, internally and in the busy, bustling marketplace.

Part of the logo concept is to encourage development of a common theme for offices and operating units, perhaps in the layout of reception and conference room facilities, of signs and notices. Visitors and staff alike then readily identify with the company.

Emphasis on a common style is also practicable for an international operation, given due sensitivity to local cultures and perceptions. The use of colour, for instance, requires care: to many American businessmen, brown is negative (and the drive of the wearer of a suit in that colour is discounted). Yellow, red and blue, in particular, carry (possibly subconscious) signals in different societies, and are to be applied only after checking. The same holds true for illustrations: using a happy piglet in an illustration or advertisement in Europe is one thing, it would be quite another to do so in the Middle East.

A successful logo helps everyone, including visitors, to identify with the style, to feel comfortable and at home; any given facet is minor but the overall effect is to convey a message of confidence and continuity.

THE ELECTRONIC NETWORK

The terminals

The linked terminals of the electronic system are the fastest-growing and rapidly becoming the main medium of operational communication.

The burgeoning databases add an ever-growing dimension to the network.

The terminal is ubiquitous. At the point of direct interface with the public, it allows access to and provision of service at optimal levels for the supplier and the customer. Internally, at the workplace, the terminal links individuals to all the in-house data necessary to carry out the specific function. It also gives access to the databases of the world, the ever-expanding universe of information.

Awareness of availability of data, of the increasingly sophisticated linkages and references, has become a skill in its own right. The historic difficulty, that of finding and capturing data, is giving way to the need to learn how to handle and absorb all that is available and then to communicate actionable information. The individual is increasingly able to devote the time to 'managing', to working creatively towards meeting the targets and objectives.

Personal usage

Open to instant access and often an object of personal rapport, the terminal is used spontaneously, even with emotion. It has become a personality extension to the point that systems are burdened by private usage, possibly at the expense of legitimate business. Pornographic and malicious use create further problems, forcing consideration of the incorporation of further checks and controls.

Undue levels of unofficial usage do raise a question: can there be a lack of communication, a feeling of personal isolation behind heavy volumes of personal messaging, the fun use of a system? Rather than a total ban on personal use, which is liable to raise personnel problems anyway, the system can be of help in auditing the effectiveness of internal communication.

Analysis of what is being said, even if frivolous, of calls for help and assistance, reveal gaps in the communication network that merit attention.

From the corporate standpoint, the electronic system is the ideal communication medium.

Usage of the internal network

The system files give updated **operational information** to the staff for each specific task. The sales people, in particular, have the latest information to hand on client organization and contacts.

- Planners and management can access all available **data on competition**, the status of individual competitors, their activities, current programmes and what is known of future plans.
- The noticeboard **announces events**, meetings, conferences, perhaps staff movements and visitor schedules.
- Internal **records and the information** held on world databases is at hand.
- While still to be further exploited for the purpose, the terminal allows management to **'talk' to the workforce**, to maintain a direct link with every desk and station, to bridge the great 'them' and 'us' divide. A periodic, even daily bulletin carries the 'family' news of events and developments to every corner of the organization. An element of this 'news' can be personal, carrying social items, staff announcements and anniversaries. People news is always assured of readership.

Japan has the interesting custom of publishing the prime minister's minute-by-minute schedule for the day, forging a link between the highest office and every home in the country. Publishing the activities of a company chief executive for each day would imply a cultural change in most organizations but at least a record of major events at senior management level could be put out on the terminals. More usually, the terminals are linked to comment and suggestion files, to a personnel question and answer service, in all creating a live in-house network.

Powerful integrated systems require the communicator to have both a sound knowledge of information technology and a wide understanding of the corporation, to be equally at home in the finance office as with the marketing team or in discussing the production cycle. From demanding information technology skills, the networks have moved on to require a new level of communication talent, one capable of exploiting the fast-developing systems to the full.

Integrated corporate systems, linked to the information superhighway, as this is defined and developed, point to network communication becoming a top skill, developing into a new recognized profession.

Expanding the external network

Externally, the systems link suppliers and customers on a world basis that is also ever-growing in sophistication. A knowledge of the market and industrial data available and an understanding of how to handle it within any given segment, is already a specialized skill. Exploitation of all the communication opportunities offered by the external network will remain a key management concern, make a continuing call on the investment budget and become increasingly important in the annual planning cycle.

At the other end of the spectrum is the remote or distributed network, with employees and consultant specialists working in 'isolation', either from home or in the marketplace, in a variety of organizational modes. A small central office can service, handle appointments, take messages, for a large number of mobile workers occupied full-time in the field.

These developments all place a greater burden on communication management. The technology has to be got right but more important is the question of whether the level of human contact is being maintained and is seen to be adequate. Most people cannot work at full efficiency for long on their own, negative feelings develop and barriers are built.

Communication management has to be sure that these aspects are recognized and probed in depth during the annual audits of the function. No assumptions can be made for it is certain that whatever the development path, there will be human difficulties. The alert network aims to expose and handle communication problems before damage is done to the organization as a whole.

Teleconferencing

The telephone conference has become a reality but has not become as significant a feature as has sometime been suggested. It may well take a new generation of managers to feel psychologically comfortable with holding discussions through the screen.

Private networks encourage use of the technique for in-house occasions, specifically in the case of international organizations whose managers need to 'meet' regularly and have the advantage of knowing each other well. Such personal acquaintance among participants is probably a requirement for the full acceptance of the teleconference. Meanwhile, the allure of travel remains strong.

The teleconference has a clear advantage in that, unlike travel and visiting, it can be accurately costed, in terms both of the actual out-of-pocket expense and of the participants' time involvement. This feature, together with the time constraints faced by leaner management teams, should encourage wider use of the medium.

The telephone

The telephone is ubiquitous, convenient and essential. However, its use does require care (discussed in Chapter 2) and, from a corporate standpoint, has a serious disadvantage: the time that is wasted on the telephone both in making unnecessary calls and more particularly, in extended conversation.

A call often starts with the social niceties and can continue with generalities for much of the time. Meanwhile, business is delayed and other contacts are kept waiting or are lost. Of course, people cannot be confined to the discussion of business alone and the telephone perhaps equals direct personal contact as a medium for the exchange of news and information, for the building of relationships.

Apart from Japan, where direct personal contact is essential, the telephone is an important, if not the main regular link with colleagues, customers, events and news. On the other hand, it is a great consumer of time, not least by its power to interrupt and distract from the task in hand.

Some jobs are virtually tied to the telephone and generalization is not possible. However, personal observation (not statistically significant!) spotlights a fair proportion of executives who, when finally at their desks and not travelling or in meetings, spend their time on the instrument. Perhaps these people form the tiers of management disappearing with 're-engineering' but, meanwhile, one impression is that if anything, their proportion is growing. Personal generalizations apart, the telephone does represent a significant cost, more indirect in the use of time than in the direct charges, and it is one given virtually no attention.

Training in telephone technique, in a disciplined approach to the instrument, deserves an emphasis that is seldom seen in office efficiency programmes. In the final analysis, control or creating some measure of awareness of telephone activity, probably requires a communication costing effort (such as suggested in Chapter 15).

The fax

The negatives of telephone usage are overcome by the fax.

The harried executive does not have to wait for a telephone connection or for dictation to be typed and checked (or even rechecked as with a telex) but can shoot a handwritten note down the line at a moment's notice.

It follows that such messages are to the point and, hopefully, unambiguous, eschewing superfluity of greeting and expression. Should an addressee be absent, it can be assumed that there are arrangements in place for the fax message to be delivered in reasonable time. There is none of the frustration and loss of time associated with aborted telephone calls, the misunderstandings that arise from poorly recorded verbal messages.

The fax is a written record not subject to the misinterpretations of the verbal and, given its speed and availability, allows an executive to tackle more of the routine directly, at any time and irrespective of the availability of supporting staff. The fax is one tool allowing a genuine increase in management productivity.

That said, it has to be kept in mind that the fax is a channel of indirect contact, of depersonalized communication. While people may misunderstand, or interpret selectively, or become antagonistic in direct discussion, most nevertheless do feel a need to meet and get to know contacts personally. Not even the most realistic of videos fills that need. For the great majority, satisfactory working arrangements are built on personal relationships and developed by regular or occasional meeting: Dante sighing endlessly for his once-seen Beatrice did not have to run a business.

THE MEDIUM OF PRINT

Internal publications

Internal communication through print is viable in any but the smallest of organizations and even then a staff circular proves helpful. While much 'news' is distributed over the electronic network, the printed word continues to have an 'atmosphere' and a permanence that keeps its value.

The successful house journal fulfils the following functions:

- It covers an individual **geographic market**. An international section can be of interest in a world corporation but attempting to cover the globe in one publication, as is sometimes the case, results in too broad a brush, offering too little of direct interest to any one group. The material then also tends to be dated and stale.
- It reports the **budget status and current forecasts**, at least to the extent that these are discussed with financial analysts. It is an

unhappy feature of corporate communication attitudes that data which are made available freely to finance houses and journalists can only be whispered in-house, are held as confidential from the very people creating and living by these results from day to day.

Useful reporting techniques include having the house magazine use an outside journalist to interview the chief executive; to summarize what has been said at the financial presentations; or simply to reprint reports on the company that have appeared in the media. Not every member of the workforce reads the financial pages and, for those who do, some amplification is always of interest.

Privately owned concerns tend to publish less than the public corporations, for no very obvious reasons other than inarticulated fears and suspicions. It has been a salutary experience for secretive European companies seeking US share quotations or capital to have had to comply with American disclosure regulations. In the case of Daimler-Benz, the German engineering giant, an operating profit in the home accounts was turned into a loss for Wall Street. The point of interest for the communicator is that the disclosures have not had a discernible effect. There is no rationale behind the common blanket fear of publication.

- It details **decisions and developments** related to the current year, the planning for the immediate future, again subjects which tend to be discussed more openly with outside interests than the workforce.
- It notes **improvements and changes** planned for products and services. There should be some indication at least of associated problems. These are often not mentioned, even when well known to the internal audience, a failure not likely to enhance trust or confidence in the management.

  No additional harm comes from mentioning a problem, discussing possible or likely solutions, and doing so may well pre-empt damaging rumour. Lack of frankness is a negative, raising a doubt as to management's grasp of events, certainly indicating a lack of respect for the employees.
- It analyses **relevant technology** both internal and as reported generally. The future is exciting and nothing but good can come from sharing it with everyone.

The business apart, house journals are designed to talk, to address the family. Personal involvement comes in such features as:

- the **individual contributions** from a department or specialist, or the recording of an achievement; reports can describe different or new market approaches or carry an outside view-point;

- staff issues, typically in the form of answers to queries, on health, pensions and the various entitlements;
- and **social news**. This is invariably a popular feature, even when somewhat dated. People like to be noticed, to have office events recorded. The reports cover personal and career landmarks, awards and outside achievements, news of pensioners and trans-ferred employees, of corporate changes and developments at head office.

Running a worth-while publication can appear an onerous task with no very obvious impact on the bottom line other than one of cost. In a period of restraint, there is a temptation in the search for economies, to dismiss the value of a magazine. The staff polls give a good indica-tion of the acceptability of what is being done (and that reaction will mainly be based on the relevancy and honesty of the contents). Cost does not have to be excessive. A reasonably competent assistant in the chief executive or personnel office, with some journalistic background or flair, and using outside professional help, can fit the task of running a quarterly publication into the routine, with marginal cost.

However, once the commitment to publish has been made, the resource does have to be available, year-in, year-out. A faltering or poor publication is self-defeating. At the same time, operating execu-tives, who have to be supportive if the venture is to be successful, are happier to contribute themselves and have their staff cooperate with a quality product than in fulfilling what is seen as a dreary duty. A successful house publication feeds on itself.

External publication

Publication of a magazine for external consumption, for clients, buyers and suppliers, is a more onerous commitment. The first and essential requirement is for the publication to carry **'real' news**, reports of direct interest to the audience, not simply good-to-know data or edit-orialized advertising.

The presentation, too, must be such as to stand out, to demand attention in the flood of material moving across the desk. In all, an external publication is a **professional commitment** and one to be carefully researched and considered before launch.

An interesting development has been that of the newsletters which have become a popular channel of communication for professional firms. Accountants and solicitors, in particular, use **newsletters** as a link with their clients and with the so-called intermediaries, the banks, financial advisers, consultants. The professional firms have one great advantage: the flow of legislation and regulation, and its interpretation, is such that there is always material of direct reader interest for these newsletters. Editorial copy does not have to be sought or bought, there is sufficient to hand.

Alternatives to individual newsletters include the insertion of a **company section** into an established publication, or buying and then personalizing a **syndicated trade or professional newsletter** with the firm's material and logo. In this way, much of the on-going editorial and production burden is removed and only matter directly related to the firm needs to be written.

The temptation of the house journal is to use it for matter that in essence is focused on what the market ought to know rather than on what it wants to know. This is a distinction requiring a degree of journalistic experience or flair that is not always available in-house. Style and the correct mix of editorial content, presented attractively, but not in too ostentatious a form for the target audience, are key to the success of a market magazine or newsheet. If one is worth doing, it is as well to place it under professional supervision.

Circulars

Internal circulars are issued on a routine basis, either on paper or through the electronic mail, to announce events or staff and organizational moves. Useful additional communication can be achieved by a regular management circular, which publishes responses to, and comments on, all the reports and material sent in to the chief executive. This is feedback on, and acknowledgement of, the value of routine communication, proof that it is being absorbed and used.

The management circular need not be an onerous task. The assistant to the president notes relevant items as the mail is cleared each day and collates these each week or, more usually once a month, into the head office summary.

The management circular carries the items in a standard format, without added comment or background, it being assumed that the recipients know the business and have no need of explanations on a routine basis. In other words, the circular does not involve editorial work or layout, it is simply a re-issue of received material. Typical sections include:

- **market developments**, the economic, structural and legal news reported by the field offices;
- **client events**, changes and new contacts;
- **product** and service developments;
- **competitive activity** and technological change.

Handled competently, the management circular is a popular link of the network. Managers who are not normally in touch hear of each other's progress, ideas are published and solutions noted. Over time, the circular becomes a source of reference, the more so if an index (readily created on the publishing desk's PC) is issued each quarter.

The noticeboard

The noticeboard is a humble tool, too often allowed to deteriorate into unsightliness, carrying dated and fly-blown material. As such it is an eyesore, one exposed to the view of staff and visitors alike, and that in a central location.

The standard notices, those on the fire and safety regulations, the warnings on security, are best printed in clear format and then framed and hung separately from the main noticeboard. Flapping, soiled sheets of emergency instruction do not encourage attention, and also destroy the noticeboard as a medium.

Good design and regular change should be a feature of the board: it is a mirror of office standards and deserves appropriate attention. It can also be useful, in publicizing vacancies, people movements of the day or week, the meetings schedule, the visitor programme, events and occasions.

The successful noticeboard is one that is the responsibility of a designated person. It helps for it to be personalized, perhaps by carrying private advertising for employees of items sought or for sale, of charity and community events being promoted by individuals.

ROUTINE REPORTING

Routing reporting broadly flows along the lines of:

- long-range plan to budget to the financial package of current (monthly or quarterly) results and weekly flash estimates;

- markets: management and agents' reports and returns;
- research: product profiles, technical assessments, market tests;
- audit: internal financial and marketing/operational assessments;

and, given managed communication, the relevant data are available via the terminals, the publications and the consultative groups.

World corporations

World corporations, possibly made up of divisions each with its own global organization, run the network by unit. There is no direct synergy between widely disparate businesses, each with its own jargon and technicalities.

Corporate results and events are, however, of concern. The interest of employees in their company at least equals, if it does not exceed, that of the shareholders and they should not have to depend on the financial pages for their information.

The average employee does not read the financial newspapers, less so those of a foreign country. An item published in the *Wall Street Journal* is not likely to reach the worker in Scotland or Germany. As surveys and actual events show, employees remain in blissful ignorance of the state of health of the employer, until difficulties arise or disaster strikes. It should then come as no surprise when the workers refuse to accept changes found essential by management and fight back by blocking an airport or infesting offices and factories.

Corporate communication personnel tend to service the information needs of the home market and of head office. The rest of the organization gets broad-brush good-to-know material, often of no particular timeliness and of only marginal interest to any one operating unit. It can be counter-productive, appearing wasteful and confirming the field's ever-present suspicion of senior management's remoteness.

Good-to-know features can be sent out as such, syndicated for local publication, but the real interest in corporate affairs lies in news of the results being achieved, of business progress and structural change. A professional director or vice-president of communication will be a listener and, it is to be hoped, will have the opportunity to do so in direct contact with operations, learning at first hand what the world audience needs and wishes to know.

It will be only too obvious what management believes to be of interest and wants to make known; the executive has to have both the authority and the judgment to achieve the right balance. It can be a delicate task but it is a disaster to be claiming 'we've never been in better shape' even while the chairman is announcing a fall in revenue or a product collapse looms. Creditability and confidence then take some little time to rebuild.

MEETINGS AND CONFERENCES

Given the scale of investment in these events, the organization of meetings and conferences deserves detailed attention. First to be recognized is the importance of the physical facilities of the meeting place. A messy room, littered with the remains of previous gatherings, communicates carelessness, low expectations, compounded when the start of proceedings is delayed while matters are put right.

Managed communication ensures that the maintenance and upkeep of the accommodation is a specific responsibility. Preparing the room, checking out the equipment, laying on supplies and refreshments, takes experience, and also time. A hurried, last-minute arrangement of the facilities shows, in breakdowns and in uncomfortable hitches. The technical organization of a major event, a conference, is a task for the professional and it is usually a false economy to use internal or dele-gated secretarial resources for any but the smallest of occasions. A lack of facilities, even as minor a point as having nowhere to hang coats, can disrupt and put matters out of tune.

The broad outlines of how meetings are to be arranged and conducted are set out in the policy manual. In general, planning starts with the issue by the organizer or sponsor of a draft agenda, followed by the allocation of each session to a coordinator. Other features to be considered include the following.

Time

Time and timing is key to a successful meeting. It is a policy require-ment that events start on time and that the agenda is followed, if necessary by firm cut-off, no matter who is involved. Time is always pressing but the experienced sponsor knows that the ability of people to absorb is limited, that there is no reward in crowding the sessions.

It is doubtful if more than two or three points can be put across in any one period, no matter how well run, and it is a good rule-of-thumb for sessions not to exceed 40 minutes. Extra material can always be made available or circulated. The optimum presentation time is probably 30 minutes, followed by ten minutes for a question or two and a five-minute break. Complex topics have to be divided into more sessions.

Informal contact

Informal contact is an important hidden benefit and recognized in the schedule. Ideally, one or two sessions are left open, with tables and rooms available to people or groups wishing to meet for purposes outside the agenda.

Mealtimes, too, can be used, by arranging for tables to be allocated to different topics or allowing specialist groups to reserve space. Buffet-style meals have the advantage of allowing people to move between groups. Fatigue is a conference negative, more so at internal events when escape is not an option, so that unhurried breaks, unstructured meals with time to take the air for a few minutes, will refresh and renew interest.

Social events

Social events can and, perhaps surprisingly, do become a burden. Arrangements are best when there is a reasonable break between the last session and assembly for the evening event. Attendance at social events is kept voluntary and, for any gathering spread over more than two nights away, each third evening is kept free, without official arrangements. Delegates appreciate being able to sample the local delights in their own way – or being free to just have an early night and go to bed.

SUMMARY

Managed communication requires the understanding and effective handling of all the mediums available.

- The logo is a focus, a symbol of identity for both the employees and public.
- The electronic system is an ideal medium, to be fully exploited internally in two-way communication.
- The use of the telephone, the fax and print is enhanced by an understanding of their capabilities and limitations.
- The humble links of circulars and noticeboards are also seen to be of value.
- Conferences and meetings are recognized as investments, to be handled professionally.

15

THE COSTING OF COMMUNICATION

Communication can be costed. Discussed here are the definitions on which to base a company-wide pro-forma budget. In turn, this is shown to be a useful analysis of the total communication effort.

INTRODUCTION

To cost communication is to:

- look at an organization from a new perspective;
- underline the value of having the function recognized as a discrete task of management.

Expenditures on major communication links, such as advertising, market research and training, are carried in the relevant budgets and can readily be pulled together. For the other elements, costing is achieved on a more subjective basis. The aim is to build a pro-forma budget, showing the cost of communication in total and by department.

The results also reveal expenditure by relevant criteria, e.g. by sales territory, and by function such as that of the personnel office, or the investment in meetings, on travel or in the electronic system.

These costs are examined piecemeal by every company, e.g. the scale of advertising is reviewed or there is a call to account for a department's travel expenditure. Managed communication aims to develop an overall perspective of the function, to allow a measure of control and to give an insight into operations from a different perspective.

DEFINITIONS

Direct expenditures

The first step of the exercise is to establish definitions. The direct expenditures are readily identified. The various advertising and market research budgets, for instance, are to hand by department or product group. These figures usually represent only the actual costs of creating and running campaigns or of paying for market research but the total investment also includes management, with related office space and facilities.

Given reasonable management financial reporting, the total cost per employee, including the overhead, is readily identifiable and the task of defining becomes one of specifying which of the staff are to be allocated, in part or wholly, to each function.

Elements of cost

Next a view is taken of the communication element of other costs held in the operating budgets, of the personnel office, of the data processing team and the electronic network, of the running of the sales force. It need not be a difficult or extensive exercise to take each operating budget and view it from the aspect of communication.

It may be held, for instance, that half the time of the personnel office overall is devoted to communication, dealing with individuals and contacting the staff generally, as opposed to managing affairs in terms of administering the arrangements of pay and entitlements, dealing with the authorities and formulating policy in the light of changing circumstances.

In the case of an information company, the electronic network will be devoted to delivering the services to clients, the communication element being relatively very small. The proportion will be somewhat higher for a manufacturer where communication will share the use of the network with such operational tasks as stockholding, accounting and technical exchange.

Intangibles

The full communication cost of other activities can be more difficult to establish. Travel expenditure is budgeted by individual and consolidation across function is necessary to get a total picture. It then becomes a matter of judgment as to what constitutes the communication element. Perhaps very little of production employee or research department travel will be considered related to communication while all of that of the advertising manager or public relations director will be allocated to the function.

Meetings are a major cost but not budgeted as such. Simply getting a view of the whole area is a valuable exercise in its own right, one that throws new light on every operation. The key question is the time involved by each employee in meetings. This is the one major cost which virtually no management seeks to manage, a great pit of unconstrained expenditure.

THE COMMUNICATION COSTS OF MANAGEMENT

The communication cost of management, including that of the senior people, is built into the pro-forma budget by allocation based on a broad analysis of activity and use of time.

The time devoted to communication by the chief executive might be defined as the periods spent outside, with the financial community and shareholders, and inside, in meetings, on facility and departmental visits. Part of his office, the central desk function, is a direct communication cost.

Such assessment is made for every executive. Clearly, the director of marketing allocates the bulk of his time to communication, the production chief relatively little. In between are such functions as accounts and distribution, the communication element of which is in part subjective judgment.

If a more factual basis is considered desirable, the definition exercise can be based on having managers log all activity for sample weeks, spaced out over half a year. The results are extrapolated, taking account of the exceptional periods when the major annual events take place. The allocation is one of full cost, that is including the relevant overheads of space and facilities.

Meetings

Meeting costs are widely spread, by individual for travel and accommodation, by host office or market for venues, or in regional and head office budgets. These direct costs can be totalled with relatively little difficulty. To give the total picture, however, it is necessary to add the cost of time spent in meetings. This element can be developed from the data input to the annual 'audit' of communication effectiveness which includes the hours spent in meetings by workers at different levels of seniority.

There will be a degree of arbitrariness in the extrapolation but, given that the base once fixed is not changed, the resulting pro-forma allows review directly within the operating year or period and also by comparison with the past. Management is able to exercise a degree of control in this diaphanous area.

Individual events are built into operating cycles and become part of accepted routine without consideration of true cost. Is every one of these occasions necessary? What savings can be made, of events or by reduced participation? Given some basis of cost, the number, frequency and structure of meetings and conferences comes into question, whether each one is the best, most effective use of time and resource.

Executives are appointed to carry out a function, run a desk, and presumably their task has to continue during absences. Are the absences cost-effective? In obverse, the value of the meetings is questioned. The annual audit apart, individual events can be assessed further by checking the minutes with participants and establishing the record of subsequent implementation.

These reviews raise interesting questions. For instance, enhanced communication between production managers, who may rarely meet, might be considered to outweigh the benefit of a marketing event that has been held routinely over the years. Overall, the effort to cost meetings and conferences puts the established operating cycle under scrutiny in a new and unfamiliar light.

Travel

Visiting, travel and entertainment is another area of communication cost so spread over budgets as not to be routinely identifiable. Total T & E expenditure periodically attracts attention and perhaps there is a call for a general reduction in percentage terms on the global figure. A published survey reported that 40% of senior executives with major American corporations had no idea of what was being spent on travel. One company that did total expenditure and arrived at a staggering sum ordered executives to fly economy and use cheaper medium-class hotels.

A saving of 25% was reported but, given past experience, the subject will sink from view when travel is examined by line management at the individual budget level. It will then be found justifiable and revert to the old level.

The advantage of a global pro-forma communication budget is that it isolates travel by function and department or office across the organization on a regular, annual basis. The cost is then related to attendance at meetings, to internal visiting, and, as appropriate, to client contact at senior level. At the minimum, study can lead to travel being coordinated, to seeking to meet more than one objective or to combine the purposes of a journey. For instance, is it necessary for the marketing director and the advertising manager both to visit each office?

Perhaps most important is the point that, once a communication pro-forma budget is prepared and becomes an established feature of the operating cycle, these elements of cost cannot be dismissed and lost to view. Travel becomes subject to the same scrutiny as does every other cost.

SALES FORCE COMMUNICATION

Communication is a significant proportion of the cost of running a sales force, itself a major element of business expense. It is made up of several strands, including training, the updating of client and market data, and the related personnel and direct management costs.

Industries run extensive training courses not only to impart product knowledge but also to heighten sales ability. The sales people then have to be supported by market and customer data. In the case of the pharmaceutical industry, for instance, the sales effort is directed at the doctor, who is the buyer of drugs in the sense of controlling all consumption through the prescription.

In order to make an impact in the few minutes a doctor usually makes available, the sales representative, or 'detailman', is armed with data in depth, on both the doctor, in terms of education, specialities and interests, and on the profile of the practice, specifically the drug consumption pattern of the area.

The performance of the rep. tends to be measured in terms of the successful introduction of a new drug, to be seen in the volume of local prescriptions, or, in obverse, maintaining a position against new products. The availability of accurate information on drug consumption is, then, a key factor in the motivation and running of the sales force.

Some of these data are generated in-house, from accounting, wholesaler and field reports, but the bulk are purchased from specialist agencies. The agencies use techniques developed over long periods for measuring the prescribing and purchase of medicines. Once collected, the data have to be handled and delivered to each representative for his or her territory, in a readily usable format, either on paper but increasingly via the electronic system.

It is a complex operation, one that makes up a significant proportion of the cost of running a pharmaceutical sales force. The direct expenses, the subscription to agency services and maintaining the electronic system, are clearly identifiable. A view has then to be taken of indirect costs. These include the time taken by each rep. in reporting back to update the data, the preparation of support materials, the expense of communicating with personnel, legal and accounting offices.

The communication cost of supporting the sales effort obviously varies: while very high in pharmaceuticals, for a small retailer it will be confined to the direct training of personnel. A charity might identify the communication cost of selling as the money spent on involving, enthusing and supporting volunteers with seminars, lectures and materials. In this case, the value to management of the analysis lies in having the ability to measure the drop-out rate, or the fund-raising result by each form of support.

Once defined, the communication cost of the sales function is included in the pro-forma budget. It becomes capable of being managed, of being weighed within the overall expenditure and against the objectives set for each cycle. The make-up of the sales force cost is seen from a new perspective.

ROUTINE OFFICE COMMUNICATION

Much of office routine can be viewed from the standpoint of expenditure on communication. The cost of an average letter is based on secretarial time, the overhead attached to each employee in terms of office space, equipment, support services. Similarly, a view can be developed for the telephone, fax, on-line link and a total built up for each department and operating unit.

One method is to calculate cost per standard unit of communication, a unit being defined as one complete message or call, irrespective of length, or as a page, or as a number of telephone units. In the immediate term, these costs are inelastic, the actual expense remaining whatever the volume of communication. However, the analysis does raise questions on the level of activity, allows comparison between operating units and over time. It questions whether a manager is over- or under-communicating with markets and colleagues.

Facilities

In practical terms, unit-of-usage analysis can produce savings. The facilities of post-room and photocopier, the fax, the telephone and terminal are usually in general overhead and cost is given only periodic if any attention. Scope for savings is revealed by comparison. Investigation of the highest cost office might, for instance, show that expenditure on the telephone can be reduced significantly by having routine messages and instructions recorded and then transmitted by automatic dial-up at off-peak rates.

This routine has the added advantage of saving people time by eliminating the social content which can make up much of routine telephone conversation.

Personnel and departmental communication

Much of the **personnel department's** expenditure, that on training, bulletins and circulars, events and ceremonies, recruitment, can well be considered communication cost.

The communication expenses of the **legal office** include the presentation and publication of new and revised regulations, such as those on insider trading or corrupt practices, and the development of corporate guidelines on, for example, the handling of contracts and third-party commitments. These are tasks additional to the handling of the company's legal affairs and are part of the pro-forma budget.

Similarly, the **accounting office** is responsible for setting standards and procedures which are communicated to every office. While routine, the costs can be above the marginal, particularly in an international operation. Other elements for the pro-forma budget are the familiarization training in accounting routines of new managers and the time devoted to advising them and attending their meetings.

Production is required to set and publicize standards and quality controls. The warehouse staff completes returns and special reports (the extent of which may be exaggerated in the hope of discouraging further bureaucratic impositions) but these are communication activities and costed for the budget.

EFFECT OF THE PRO-FORMA BUDGET

The pro-forma budget allows line-by-line scrutiny of communication by unit, office and operational area. Initially, the novelty of the concept helps to mitigate criticism of what can be seen as academic or bureaucratic interference. Once the budget is established, managers appreciate the ability to examine activity from an unconventional standpoint, the consumption of communication resource. The pro-forma shows them the cost both of the inward flow of data and intelligence and of their unit's written and verbal output.

In the case of the sales force, for instance, there is the cost of the supporting accountancy and personnel functions and of the market research data. In turn, the sales office has the cost of meeting accountancy requirements and of collecting field intelligence.

More broadly, there is the annual round of outside and industry events, attendance at which is justified in the relevant budgets by 'vested interests' but which the pro-forma budget allows to be examined in the light of results and the general interest.

Travel is part of the organizational fabric but availability of full costings, not simply the actual expenditure on fares and accommodation, acts as a spur to objective review. Results of events are weighed against alternatives or savings. The 'audit' of travel may result in additional and unpopular procedures but, even for senior managers, the controls once established, become as routine as other financial checks.

Hidden costs and links

Most importantly, the pro-forma brings to light previously hidden claims on time and resource. Most prominent will be the review of meetings and conferences. In turn this leads on to more fundamental questioning of functions. Why are the meetings being held, can the results be measured, should some people be meeting more often?

Looking elsewhere, it can be found, for instance, that the legal department has, unconsciously, attracted additional work and is making what are in fact commercial decisions. Managers have found it convenient to obtain and act on advice rather than work out problems through the more rigorous questioning built into line procedures. The pattern of communication can reveal links and decision-making that differ materially from the organization chart, showing that a given function has assumed undue importance. For instance, the cash management procedures set by the company controller have been known to over-ride commercial decisions without senior management being fully aware of the implications.

On the other hand, research and development may show minimal expenditure on communication, raising questions as to the isolation of the function from colleagues, the market. Perhaps the scientists and engineers are working to a set programme and feel no need to communicate further but it is a rare situation in which ideas are generated without continuing exchange.

The pro-forma budget helps management to get the balance right between the functions and to weigh expenditure with results.

Cost effectiveness

A study undertaken by the Kent local government council in Britain revealed that while one-third of all employees recorded dissatisfaction in some way with their jobs, over half claimed that communication to them from the authority was poor.

In commenting on the result, the council expressed the view that the cost of the survey would be covered 100 times if staff effectiveness could be increased by just 1%. General efficiency apart, better communication would also improve staff recruitment and retention, two other key concerns.

The value of listening, the basis of effective communication, is much enhanced by the development of a pro-forma budget: listening clarifies needs and sets objectives, the budget reveals what is happening in practice. There is a powerful story in the process. The initial analyses and defining necessary for the construction of the pro-forma do take effort but once done, the exercise fits into the routine and further marginal cost is minimal.

Clearly, communication is one task that is never complete or fully satisfactory: however good the story or sound the programme there will always be those not convinced and, even more challenging, the great outside, where there is always further great potential still to be contacted and persuaded. On the other hand, lack of interest in, or loss of the ability to communicate, to ignore its necessity, does have a proven result – collapse.

Communication is worthy of continuous attention. In turn, once recognized as a discrete function, communication will continue to fascinate all those involved in its unending process of change and development.

SUMMARY

The communication pro-forma budget is built on:

- clearly identified costs, such as advertising and market research;
- the communication cost of maintaining each function, e.g. the sales force, and of the input to and output from office and unit;
- analysis of expenditure on meetings, travel and visiting.

The result is to open a new viewpoint from which to scrutinize a major area of expense, consumption of the communication resource. The budget makes possible the critical examination of major categories of cost across the organization, e.g. the full expenditure, including time and overhead, on travel overall and by unit, the optimal use of communication by office and operation.

INDEX